SpeakEasy Sp..

SURVIVAL SPANISH
FOR CHURCHES
AND
MISSION TRIPS

Myelita Melton, MA

SpeakEasy Communications, Incorporated

Survival Spanish for Churches and Mission Trips

Author: Myelita A. Melton
Cover Design: Ellen Wass Beckerman
Published by SpeakEasy Communications, Incorporated
116 Sea Trail Drive
Mooresville, NC 28117-8493
USA

ISBN-10:   0-97869-989-0
ISBN-13:   978-0-97869-986-4

Using This Material

SpeakEasy Spanish for Churches and Mission Trips is the newest edition to the SpeakEasy Spanish™ series from SpeakEasy Communications, Inc. This book is designed for adults with no previous experience in the Spanish language. Wherever possible, we have chosen to use the similarities between English and Spanish to facilitate your success.

Throughout the book, you will find study tips and pronunciation guides that will help you to say the Spanish words correctly. In the guides, we have divided the Spanish words by syllable, choosing English words that closely approximate the required Spanish sound. When you see letters that are **BOLD** in the guide, say that part of the word the loudest. The bold capital letters are there to show you where the emphasis falls for that word.

At SpeakEasy Communications, we believe that *communication* is more important than *conjugation*, and that what you learn must be practical for what you do. We urge you to set realistic, practical goals. Make practice a regular part of your day and you will be surprised at the progress you make! For more information, visit us online at www.SpeakEasySpanish.com.

TABLE OF CONTENTS

SpeakEasy's Secrets to Learning Spanish

Congratulations on your decision to learn Spanish for your upcoming mission trip to Latin America. By learning and using Spanish on your journey, you will gain the trust and respect of your church's mission community—no matter where in Latin America it is. Even speaking a few words of Spanish will uplift you and give you the tools to develop meaningful friendships that will last a lifetime.

Learning Spanish is going to open many doors for you at home and abroad. In addition to feeling more comfortable on your mission trip, now you will be able to make new Spanish-speaking church members at your church feel even more welcome. You are going to raise your communication skills and cultural awareness to a whole new level.

As an adult, learning a new language requires a certain mindset. It takes time, patience, and more than a little stubbornness. It took all of us many years to learn English. When you cry for the first time just after you are born, communication begins. Later you utter syllables. When you begin to speak, your parents praise you and reward you. After a few years, you start forming simple sentences. By the time you reach kindergarten, you can't stop  talking...and it took you five years to get there. Consequently, you can't expect to speak Spanish fluently by studying it for only a few weeks. You keep at it, just like you did when you were learning English.

It's also important for you to realize that adults learn languages differently than children do. Kids learn by listening and by imitating. For them, learning Spanish or any other second language is relatively easy because their brains learn naturally. It's part of human development.

When you reach puberty and everything changes! Your body sets your speech pattern for its native language. For many people, this is the age when their language learning center slows down or turns completely off. Your body just figures it doesn't need it any longer. Coincidentally, this slow-down occurs about the same time that you hit your seventh grade Spanish class. That's why learning Spanish seemed to be so hard — that, and the huge amount of very impractical things you were forced to learn. As a result of this physical change in puberty, adults tend to learn languages more visually. However, listening and imitating are still important, especially when paired with a visual cue. Most adults benefit from seeing a Spanish word spelled phonetically and hearing it at the same time. This combination helps your brain make sense of the new sounds.

Adults are practical learners. If there is a reason for what you are studying, learning the material will be easier. It is also very true that if you practice your developing Spanish skills daily, you are less likely to forget them. Yes, you can teach an old dog new tricks! You are never too old to learn Spanish.

If you did take Spanish in high school or college, you are going to be pleasantly surprised when words and phrases you thought you had forgotten begin to come back to you. That previous experience with other languages is still in your mind. It's just hidden away in a seldom used filing cabinet. Soon

Here's another thought for you to consider. What you learned in the traditional foreign language classroom is not exactly correct.

There's no such thing as "perfect Spanish" just as there is no such thing as "perfect English."

All native speakers make mistakes. We are only human! This fact leaves the door for good communication wide open! If you wait until you have the "perfect" sentence formed with all the verbs conjugated correctly, along with every little "el" and "las" in the right place, you will never say anything to anyone. No one who speaks Spanish is going to give you a grade. So, please stop worrying about perfection and start talking!

The secret to learning Spanish is having self-confidence and a good sense of humor. To build self-confidence, you must realize that the entire learning experience is painless and fun. Naturally, you are going to make mistakes — everyone does. We all make mistakes in English too! So get ready to laugh and to learn.

This is extremely important: Don't think that you must have a perfect Spanish sentence in your head before you say anything. Say what you know—even if it's only a word or two. The point is to communicate. Communication doesn't have to be "pretty" or perfect to be effective!

Spanish is one of the world's most precise, lyrical, and expressive languages. Consider these other important facts as you begin to "*habla español*":

- English and Spanish share a common Latin heritage, so literally thousands of words in our two languages are either similar or identical.

- Your ability to communicate is the most important thing, so your grammar and pronunciation don't have to be "perfect" for you to be understood.

- Some very practical and common expressions in Spanish can be communicated with a few simple words.

- Saying even a phrase or two in Spanish every day will help you learn faster.

- Relax! People who enjoy their learning experiences acquire Spanish at a much faster pace than others.

- Set realistic goals and establish reasonable practice habits.

- When you speak even a little Spanish, you are showing a tremendous respect for the Hispanic culture and its people.

- Even a little Spanish or *poco español* goes a long way!

As you begin the process of learning Spanish, you are going to notice a few important differences. Speaking Spanish is going to feel and sound a little odd to you at first. This feeling is completely normal; you are using muscles in your face that English doesn't require and your inner ear is not accustomed to hearing you speak Spanish. People tell me it sounds and feels like a cartoon character has gotten inside your head! Don't let that stop you. Just keep right on going! The more you practice, the more natural Spanish will feel and sound to you.

4

The Sounds of Spanish

The most important sounds in Spanish consist of *five* vowels. Each one is pronounced the way it is written. Spanish vowels are never *silent*. Even if there are two vowels together in a word, both of them will stand up and be heard.

A	(ah)	as in mama
E	(eh)	as in "hay or the "eh" in set
I	(ee)	as in deep
O	(oh)	as in open
U	(oo)	as in spoon

Here are the other sounds you'll need to remember. Always pronounce them the same way.

Spanish Letter	**English Sound**
C	(before e or i) s as in Sam: **cero:** SAY-row
G	(before e or i) h as in he: **energía:** n-air-HE-ah **emergencia:** a-mare-HEN-see-ah
H	silent: **hacienda:** ah-see-N-da
J	h as in hot: **Julio,** HOO-lee-oh
LL	y as in yoyo: **tortilla,** tor- TEE-ya
Ñ	ny as in canyon: **español,** es-pan- NYOL
QU	k as in kit: **tequila,** tay-KEY-la
RR	Trilled r sound: **burro,** BOO-row
V	v as in Victor: **Victor,** Vic-TOR
Z	s as in son: **Gonzales,** gone-SA-les

5

Note: People from Latin American countries have a variety of accents just like people do in the United States. In certain areas of Latin America, people tend to pronounce the letter "v" more like the English letter "b." In other Latin American countries, a "v" sounds like an English "v." If you learned to switch the "v" sound for a "b" sound in other Spanish classes, don't change your habit; however, if you have had no experience with Spanish before now, don't sweat the small stuff! Pronounce the "v" as you normally do.

The Other Consonants: The remaining letters in Spanish have very similar sounds to their equivalent in English.

The Spanish Alphabet
El alphabeto español

A	ah	J	HO-ta	R	AIR-ray
B	bay	K	ka	RR	EH-rray
C	say	L	L-ay	S	S-ay
CHE	chay	LL	A-yea	T	tay
D	day	M	M-ay	U	oo
E	EH or A	N	N-ay	V	vay
F	F-ay	Ñ	N-yea	W	DOE-blay-vay
G	hay	O	oh	X	A-kees
H	AH-chay	P	pay	Y	ee-gree-A-gah
I	ee	Q	coo	Z	SAY-ta

Did you notice something different about the Spanish alphabet? It has four letters the English alphabet doesn't have. Can you find them?

The Four "Extra" Letters

Look carefully at the table on the preceding page which contains the Spanish alphabet Spanish has more letters in its alphabet than English does, but none of them will present *problemas* for you. Here are the four extra letters and words in which they are used:

CH   Sounds like the following English words: Chuck, Charlie and chocolate.

LL   Sounds essentially like an English "y." However, you will hear slight variations depending on where the person who is speaking Spanish to you is originally from. Example: Tortilla (tor-T-ya)

Ñ   Sounds like a combination of "ny" as in canyon or onion: Example: *español* (es-pan-**NYOL**)

RR   This letter is a "trilled. Practice by taking your tongue and placing it on the roof of your mouth behind your front teeth. Now blow air across the tip of your tongue and make it flutter. This sound can be difficult to make. It's only strange because you are moving your tongue in a new way. Since there are no words in English with trilled sounds, you just never learned to move your tongue that way! Don't let a problem with the trilled "r" stop you from speaking. Essentially the sounds of the English "r" and the Spanish "r" are the same. To start, say the double "r" a bit louder than a single "r." Example: Burrito (boo-**REE**-toe)

The Spanish Accent

In Spanish, you will see two types of accent marks. Both marks are very important and do different things. One of the marks you will notice is called a "tilde." It is only found over the letter "N." But, don't get the Ñ confused with N. The accent mark over Ñ turns it into a different letter entirely. In fact, it's one of four letters in the Spanish alphabet that the English alphabet doesn't have. The Ñ changes the sound of the letter to a combination of "ny." You'll hear the sound that this important letter makes in the English words "canyon" and "onion."

Occasionally you will see another accent mark over a letter in a Spanish word. The accent mark or "slash" mark shows you where to place vocal emphasis. So, when you see an accent mark over a letter in a Spanish word, just say that part of the word louder. For example: José (ho-SAY). These accented syllables are indicated in our pronunciation guides with bold, capital letters.

Pronouncing Spanish Words

The pronunciation of Spanish words follows very basic, consistent rules. This regular pattern makes the language easier to learn. These are the main points to remember:

Most Spanish words that end with a vowel are stressed or emphasized on the *next to the last* syllable.

Señorita: sen-your-**REE**-ta   Jalapeño: ha-la-**PAIN**-yo

Next, look for an accent mark. If the Spanish word has an accent in it, that's the emphasized syllable.

José: ho-**SAY**   ¿Cómo está?: **KO**-mo es-**TA**

Words that end in consonants are stressed on the *final* syllable.   Doctor: doc-**TOR**   Hotel: oh-**TELL**

Spanish Punctuation Marks

Spanish has two unusual looking punctuation marks. They are used to signal you that something other than a simple declarative sentence is just ahead.

First, there's the upside down question mark (¿). You will see it at the beginning of all questions. It's there simply to let you know that what follows is a question and you will need to give your voice an upward inflection. It's the same inflection we use in English.

Example: Do you speak English?   ¿Habla inglés?

Second, there's the upside down exclamation mark (¡). It lets you know that what follows should be vocally emphasized.

Example: Hi!   ¡Hola!

Tips and Techniques for Comunicación

When you begin speaking Spanish, it's important to remember that *patience is a virtue*! Here are some easy things you can do to make your conversation flow.

✓ Speak slowly and distinctly.

✓ Do not use slang expressions or colorful terms.

✓ Get straight to the point! Unnecessary words cloud your meaning.

✓ Speak in a normal tone. Speaking *loudly* doesn't help anyone understand you any better!

✓ Look for visual cues in body language and facial expressions. Use gestures of your own to get your point across.

✓ You may not receive good eye contact. Do not interpret the lack of eye contact negatively. Eye contact varies from culture to culture.

✓ Given that Latinos tend to stand closer to each other than North Americans when they talk to each other, your personal space could feel crowded. Stand your ground!

Watch what you say and how you say it! You are an ambassador for your church, your faith and your community! One slip of the tongue could cause a world of trouble!

Beginning Words & Phrases

Let's get started! The members of your congregation and those you meet on mission trips will be delighted you are learning to speak *español*. Even if you can't remember a whole phrase, *por favor* always use the words you know.

English	Español	Guide
Hi!	¡Hola!	OH-la
How are you?	¿Cómo está?	KO-mo es-TA
Fine	Muy bien.	mooy b-N
So so	Así así	ah-SEE ah-SEE
Bad	Mal	mal
Good morning	Buenos días	boo-WAY-nos DEE-ahs
Good afternoon	Buenas tardes	boo-WAY-nas TAR-days
Good night	Buenas noches.	boo-WAY-nas NO-chase
Sir or Mister	Señor	sen-YOUR
Mrs. or Ma'am	Señora	sen-YOUR-ah
Miss	Señorita	sen-your-REE-ta
What's your name?	¿Cómo se llama?	KO-mo say YA-ma
My name is ___	Me llamo ___	may YA-mo
Nice to meet you	¡Mucho gusto!	MOO-cho GOO-stow
Thank you	Gracias.	GRA-see-ahs
Please	¡Por favor!	pour-fa-VOR

English	Español	Guide
You're welcome.	De nada.	day NA da
The pleasure is mine.	El gusto es mío.	l GOO-stow es ME-oh
Excuse me.	¡Perdón!	pear-DON
Good-bye	Adiós	ah-dee-OS

Spanish Sounds Rápido — What Do I Do Now?

Be honest! One of the reasons you are hesitant to speak Spanish is that the language sounds so fast! Naturally you're afraid you won't understand what is being said to you, and *sometimes you won't!* That's normal and natural! When you feel a little out of your depth, use these phrases to take back conversational control.

English	Español	Guide
I don't understand.	No comprendo.	no com-PREN-doe
Do you understand?	¿Comprende?	com-PREN-day
I speak a little Spanish.	Hablo poco español.	AH-blow POE-co es-pan-NYOL
Do you speak English?	¿Habla inglés?	AH-bla eng-LACE
Repeat please.	Repita por favor	ray-PETE-ah pour fa-VOR
Speak more slowly please.	Habla más despacio por favor.	AH-bla mas des-PA-see-oh pour fa-VOR

12

English	Español	Guide
Thanks for your patience.	Gracias por su paciencia.	GRA-see-ahs pour sue pa-see-N-see-ah
How do you say it in Spanish?	¿Cómo se dice en español?	CO-mo say DEE-say n es-pan-NYOL
Where are you from?	¿De dónde es?	day DON-day es

The key here is <u>not</u> to pánico.
Your Spanish-speaking your friend is having just as much trouble understanding you, as you are having understanding them! Hang in there! Between the two of you, *comunicación* will begin to take place.

Why Does Spanish Sound So Fast?

To people who speak English as their native language, the Spanish language sounds extremely fast. There are several reasons for this astute observation. First, Spanish flows from one word to another without an obvious pause between words. Sometimes it appears that native speakers only pause when they need to breathe! As a result of this gliding from word to word, it's difficult for many beginners to distinguish where one word starts and another word stops. This fact alone is a great reason to put the phrase "speak more slowly please" (*Habla más despacio, por favor.*) at the top of your "to learn" list. By using this phrase, the person you are talking to will become more conscious of their verbal speed. They will say words more slowly, and you'll begin to hear the words more distinctly.

13

Another important reason Spanish why sounds like a star ship at warp speed is that pronouns (*see chart p. 16*) are often omitted. Why? People who speak Spanish are listening for the ending of the verb in the sentence to tell them who or what is being talked about. Each verb ending is different, so it's easy to tell one from another. Native speakers of the Spanish language aren't taking their cues to meaning from pronouns at all. In this aspect of language, English and Spanish are very different. Since the pronouns aren't necessary much of the time for precise communication in Spanish, many native speakers routinely omit them.

When you compare how basic verbs sound in English and Spanish, you will realize that many regular English verbs in the present tense sound exactly the alike. Here's a good example: I speak, you speak, we speak, they speak, etc. If it weren't for the pronoun at the beginning of the sentence, we wouldn't know what or who was being talked about at all because the verbs are identical! Since many of the verbs forms sound the same, people who speak English are listening for the pronoun at the beginning of the sentence to tell them what's being discussed.

If you have studied Spanish previously, you might have learned how to ask this basic question "how are you" as *¿Cómo está <u>usted</u>?* This form includes the pronoun "*usted*." It's important to realize you may never hear it said that way in the "real world." Both *¿Cómo está usted?* and *¿Cómo está?* mean exactly the same thing. One form isn't better than the other or more polite. So, it's OK to drop those pronouns. In fact, when you do drop them, you begin to sound more natural, and as an added bonus, you'll make fewer mistakes!

14

English	Español	Guide
I	Yo	yo
You (informal)	Tú	too
He	Él	L
She	Ella	A-ya
You (Polite)	*Usted	oo-STED
We	Nosotros	no-SO-tros
	**Nosotras *(f)*	no-SO-tras
They	Ellos	A-yos
	**Ellas *(f)*	A-yas
You (Plural)	Ustedes	oo-STED-es

Tips and Tidbits

If you learned Spanish in high school, what you studied was possibly Castilian Spanish which is spoken in Spain. That type of Spanish has several different features from the language as it is spoken in Latin America. One of the unique features of Castilian Spanish is the use of the word *vosotros (-as)* or the polite form of "you." In Latin America, this form is not used. The pronoun *usted* is used instead. In this book we are concentrating on Latin American Spanish because that's what you are most likely to hear and use.

15

Which "You" Are You?
Tú or Usted

Review the table of pronouns on the preceding page. Did you notice that there are many different ways to say "you"? The pronoun *"you"* is one of the most important ones on the entire list. You will use it often, and when you do, you will have several decisions to make.

First, there is the choice of using either the Castilian or Latin American forms: *vosotros* or *usted*. We've already decided to go with Latin American Spanish since it's what you are most likely to hear in the workplace.

Next, we must decide whether it's best to be informal or more polite when we address patients and their families. On the job which should you choose *tú* or *usted*? If you studied Spanish in high school or college, you might be more comfortable using *tú*. In your classroom setting where you and your friends were the same age and on a first name basis, *tú* was the correct way to go. Because you used it so much in school, it might be the word that comes into your mind first now.

Now your needs are different and your situation has changed. In SpeakEasy Spanish™ we emphasize the need for courtesy in every phrase and form we present. Spanish is a language that is designed to show ultimate courtesy and respect, so let's use that to our advantage. In the workplace with adults *usted* is the correct form of address to use. Many Latin Americans, especially older ones, are uncomfortable with using a professional's first name quickly. For Spanish-speaking adults to move from addressing each other with *usted* to the use of *tú*, a long-term relationship must be established. Later on when you begin to work with verbs, you will also see the verb

16

form which matches *usted* is simpler to use. By using *usted*, you can't go wrong. You'll be showing courtesy and respect to your patients, and decreasing your chances of making errors in your verbs. *¡Fantástico!*

Spanish Nouns
Can words really have a gender?

¡Sí! Spanish belongs to the "romance" language family. Calling Spanish a "romance" language doesn't mean that it has anything to do with love. Where Spanish is concerned, it's all about the ancient Romans. Like many European languages, Spanish is an offshoot of Latin. Classification of nouns into groups or categories remains a common feature of each language in the romance language group today.
In ancient times, people had even more challenges learning another language than we do today. There were no tapes, CDs, or internet and few foreign language teachers. For that matter, there weren't many schools either! Most folks simply learned other languages through time consuming trial and error.

To help the challenging process along, words were placed into categories based upon how they sounded. This process organized the material and made words easier to learn. These categories were often described as "masculine," "feminine," or even "neuter." From these descriptions, people began talking about words in terms of their gender. Even though the word "gender" is misleading, the tendency to group words by sound helped people learn more quickly.

Because Spanish evolved from Latin, it has maintained two category divisions for centuries. The categories are called

17

masculine and feminine. Even though Spanish can and will evolve as all languages do, the concept of "gender" categories in español is not likely to change.

Here are the most important points to remember about nouns and their categories:

1. Usually, words are grouped by how they sound, not by what they mean. There will always be a few exceptions!
2. Languages are a lot like the people who use them: They don't always follow the rules!
3. If the Spanish noun is referring to a person, the letter will often indicate the sex of that individual. For example: a doctor, who is a man, is a "doctor" Awoman, who is a doctor, is a "doctora."
4. Words in the "masculine" category usually end with the letter "O".
5. Words in the "feminine" category usually end with the letter "A".
6. El, la, los and las are very important words. They all mean "the". They are the clues you need to tell you a word's category.

Articles: Making Connections

The words in Spanish that mark which category a noun falls into are some of the most commonly used words in the entire Spanish language. These words are called "articles." In English these are the words the, a, or an. You'll not only hear them often in Spanish, you'll use them often too.

Nouns and their articles match each other like identical twins. Here's how it works. Match the category of article and noun as either masculine or feminine. Then, determine if the noun you are using is singular or plural.

Even though the correct use of articles is an important feature of Spanish, nothing is more important than the noun! If you are unsure about which article to use, simply leave it out. The noun you say carries all the meaning. In the grand scheme of things, this mistake is relatively minor. It's much more important to say the word that carries the meaning than the word that indicates category and number. Eliminating the article on occasion or using the wrong one won't prevent you from being understood. You might not be perfect in your grammar usage, but you will be effective in your communications. Always remember: *Everyone makes mistakes—even native speakers!*

Definite and Indefinite Articles

English	Español	Guide
The (singular)	*El (m)	L
	La (f)	la
The (plural)	Los	los
	Las	las
A or an	Un (m)	oon
	Una (f)	OO-na
Some (plural)	Unos	OO-nos
	Unas	OO-nahs

19

A Word about Adjectives

Describing things in Spanish can present problems for English speakers. There are several reasons why using adjectives may give us trouble.

First, there is the position of the adjective in relation to the noun. In English, descriptive words go in front of the noun like "white cat," for example. In Spanish, the noun is the most important element, so it comes first. White cat is *gato blanco*. It is the opposite of our word order. However, it gets more complicated because there are a few basic adjectives which show size or quantity that are placed in front of the noun, just as in English. These include words like large (*grande*) and small (*pequeño*), along with numbers.

For example: a large white cat is *un grande gato blanco*. Second, since Spanish nouns are divided into masculine and feminine categories, the adjective must match its noun by category. This means that from time to time you will need to match the letter at the end of the adjective and make it the same letter that is at the end of the noun. You must also match the adjective to the noun by number (singular or plural). This matching sound feature of Spanish is one of the main reasons it has such a musical sound.

For example:

One large white cat	*Uno grande gato blanco*
Three large white cats	*Tres grandes gatos blancos*
One large white house	*Una grande casa blanca*
Six large white houses	*Seis grandes casas blancas*

Adding Description with Adjectives

These common adjectives are shown as you would find them in a Spanish dictionary. Usually the masculine form of the word is what you find in the dictionary. Often you will see (a) written after the word to indicate the feminine form.

As indicated in the table below, use the adjectives without changing their ending when you pair them with singular words in the masculine category. You will place most of these adjectives behind the noun instead of in front of it.** Change the "o" at the end of the adjective to an "a" if you need it to match a word which is feminine in category. If the adjective ends with the letter "e," you won't need to change anything to make it feminine! Also, don't forget to add an "s" at the end of your adjective to match it with plural words.

** Position adjectives which indicate a quantity, number or size in front of the noun instead of behind it.

For example: The two houses = Las dos casas
                A large meal = Una grande comida

English	Español	Guide
Good	Bueno	boo-WAY-no
Bad	Mal	mal
Big	Grande	GRAN-day
Little	Pequeño	pay-CANE-yo
More	Más	mas
Less	Menos	MAY-nos
Hot	Caliente	ca-lee-N-tay

Yours, Mine or Ours

Where is **your** son? **My** son is in high school. Notice the words in bold face type. Each of them is a possessive adjective. Now that you understand the basics about adjectives and their relationship to nouns in Spanish, let's move on to adjectives which indicate possession. They may be the easiest for you to learn and use correctly immediately.

Possessive adjectives are easy to use in Spanish for two basic reasons.
1. They come in front of the noun like they do in English.
2. Possessive adjectives do not show the gender or category of the noun they are paired with.

These common adjectives only show that the noun they are paired with is singular or plural. That makes them not only easy to use, but practical to use as well. You will be able to use them almost immediately.

English	Español	Guide
My	Mi	me
	Mis	meese
Your	Tu	too
	Tus	toos
His, her or Your (*polite*)	Su	sue
	Sus	seus
Our	Nuestro (-os)	new-**ES**-tro
	Nuestra (-as)	new-**ES**-tra

Using Adjectives to Differentiate

Adjectives are the great character actors of the language stage. They play many vital roles by putting on different faces and costumes to give us a variety of linguistic details. They certainly spice up our speech! Along with nouns and verbs, adjectives provide a powerful foundation for basic conversation.

The primary function of any adjective is to describe, but they often do much more than that. Adjectives can indicate whether an object belongs to us or someone else, and they can also be used to point out or differentiate one object from another. For example, you'll use this set of adjectives to say "**this** food is good for you" or "**that** food is high in cholesterol." Demonstrative adjectives make a practical addition to your growing vocabulary, and they are easy to use.

Demonstrative adjectives, like other adjectives in Spanish, are paired with a noun according to its gender or category and its plurality. Note that the feminine forms of these adjectives all have the letter "a" near the end of the word. That's a good indicator that you will pair it with a noun that's feminine in category. All the plural forms of demonstrative adjectives end with the letter "s." Use them when you are pointing out more than one thing.

Where location is concerned, place your demonstrative adjective directly before the noun. It takes the same spot in front of the noun just as it does in English.

Point It Out: Using Adjectives to Demonstrate

English	Español	Guide
This	Este	ES-tay
	Esta	ES-ta
That	Ese	ES-a
	Esa	ES-ah
These	Estos	ES-toes
	Estas	ES-tas
Those	Esos	ES-ohs
	Esas	ES-ahs
That one over there	Aquel	ah-**KEL**
	Aquellos	ah-**KAY**-yos
	Aquella	ah-**KAY**-ya
	Aquellas	ah-**KAY**-yas

Giving Colorful Commentary

Another important category of adjectives is vocabulary related to colors. These will come in handy in any conversational setting. You can talk about the color of clothes, plants, foods—and these words are very easy to use because you many already know many of them.

Since these adjectives do not show possession or demonstrate one from another, they follow the same rules that the majority of adjectives do in Spanish. Remember to position them after the noun they describe. Colors must also "agree" with their nouns in two different ways. First, the color and its accompanying noun must agree by category: masculine or feminine. If the noun ends with the letter "o" and is masculine in category, change the ending of the color to an "o." For feminine nouns, make sure to change the ending of your adjective to an "a."

Next, your colors and nouns must agree in number: singular or plural. This is done by simply adding the letter "s" to the color so that it matches the plural ending (-s or –es) on the noun.

Tips & Tidbits
The colors used in homes and churches in Latin America are more likely to be brighter more tropical ones than most of us choose in the US.

Los Colores

English	Español	Guide
Black	Negro	NAY-grow
Blue	Azul	ah-SOOL
Brown	Moreno	mo-RAY-no
Gray	Gris	grease
Green	Verde	VER-day
Orange	Naranja	na-RAHN-ha
Pink	Rosa	ROW-sa
Purple	Morado	mo-RAH-do
Red	Rojo	ROW-ho
White	Blanco	BLAHN-co
Yellow	Amarillo	ah-ma-REE-yo

What Is Your Complete Name?
¿Cuál es su nombre completo?

Hispanic Names Have Four Important Parts

First Name	Middle Name	Father's Surname	Mother's Surname
Primer Nombre	Segundo Nombre	Apellido Paterno	Apellido Materno
Carlos	Juan	Santana	Rodríguez
Ramón	Marco	Villarosa	Cruz
Carmen	Elena	Miranda	Rivera

One of the most common errors in recording Hispanic names involves an incorrect understanding of their order. Many Hispanic "full" or "complete" names contain four parts: a first name, a middle or "second" name, and two family surnames.

The surname from an individual's paternal side is normally third in order. It is the correct choice for "last name" on forms instead of the name in the actual last position. Look at the table containing names above. Santana, Villarosa, and Miranda are the correct choice for "last name." In many facilities both names are required. If that is the case in your institution, both names would be listed under last name. When alphabetizing, the third or paternal name would be used. Do not insert an unnecessary hyphen between a man's *apellido paterno* and *apellido materno*. Hyphens are used in a married woman's name to show the linking of the two families. When addressing a Hispanic gentleman, it's correct to use either the *apellido paterno* alone or both family surnames.

Women:

A woman's name follows the same order and only changes upon marriage. When a single woman marries, she drops her *apellido materno* or "maiden" name. It is replaced by the *apellido paterno* of her husband.

Look closely at the following example:

Carmen Elena Miranda Rivera has married Carlos Juan Santana Rodríguez. She will now drop the use of her *apellido materno* which is "Rivera." She will add her husband's *apellido paterno* "Santana." Most women link their apellido paterno and their husbands with a hypen. Her name is now Carmen Miranda-Santana.

Children:

Let's explore the family of Carlos Santana and Carmen Miranda-Santana further by examining the name of their son Juan Luis. Just as Carmen and Carlos do, their son will have a first and second name. Those are Juan and Luis. He also has two family surnames, one from his father and one from his mother. Their son's surname order would be Santana Miranda. Santana is his *apellido paterno* and Miranda is his *apellido materno*. His full or complete name is Juan Luis Santana Miranda.

Full Name or Complete Name?

In any language there are usually at least three or four different ways to say just about anything you want to say. Both in Spanish and in English, there are at least three different ways to ask a person for their name. Here are the three most common ways to ask for this important bit of information:

1. *¿Cómo se llama?*
2. *¿Cuál es su nombre?*
3. *¿Cuál es su nombre completo?*

If you choose option one, you are likely to receive only the individual's first name. Why? Because *cómo se llama* literally means "how do you call yourself. It does *not* mean what is your name.

Choice number two means what is your name, but, you are *still* not asking for the "whole enchilada"! Again, the person may only give you their name.

By using choice number three, you are asking for the person's full or complete name. In Spanish a person's entire name is always his or her "complete" name. It's never considered to be a "full" name. That's because for your name to technically be "full," it would also have to be the opposite of that or empty! Since your name doesn't hold water like a cup or food like your stomach does, your name can't possibly be full. Your name is a piece of information, so it's considered to be either complete or incomplete. "*Completo*" is also a stronger match to the English word complete, making it much easier to use!

The Essentials of Spanish Verbs

There are basically three types of regular verbs in Spanish. The last two letters on the end of the verb determines how the word is to be treated. Listed below are the three most common types of regular verb endings.

AR – Hablar: To speak
ER – Comprender: To understand
IR – Escribir: To write

In SpeakEasy Spanish™, we focus on speaking about ourselves and talking to another person. That's the most common type of "one-on-one" communication.

When you need to say "I speak," "I understand," or "I live," change the last two letters of the verb to an "O".

Hablo
Comprendo
Escribo

When asking a question such as "do you speak," "do you understand," or "do you live," change the ending to an "a" or an "e".

> *The change in letter indicates that you are
> speaking to someone else.*

Habla
Comprende
Escribe

To make a sentence negative, simply put "no" in front of the verb.

No hablo.
No comprendo.
No escribo.

¡Acción!

There are so many English friendly *acción* words in the Spanish "AR" verb family. Many of them bear a strong resemblance to English verbs — most of them share a simple, regular nature. They are a very important asset in on-the-job communication. We picked a few of our favorites to get you started. Look closely at the list on the next page. On it, you will recognize many comforting similarities between our languages that are also practical! Changing one letter will really expand your conversational skills.

In on-the-job conversations, people tend to use "I" and "you" to start many sentences. Of all the pronouns, these two are the most powerful and will work best for you, so that's where we will start.

Here's an important difference between our languages — in English, the use of pronouns is essential because most of our verbs tend to end the same way. For example, with "I speak" and "you speak" the verb "speak" remains the same. In English, our pronouns make all the difference. Spanish is different in this aspect. Spanish-speaking people are listening for the letters at the end of the verb. That's what indicates who or what is being talked about in Spanish. Each ending is different. The ending of the Spanish verb is much more important than the beginning. The ending of the verb tells the Spanish-speaking person who, or what, is being discussed. In most cases when people speak Spanish, you might not hear a pronoun. It's not necessary for precise meaning. That's a big reason why Spanish might sound a little fast to you:

Pronouns which are important in English are routinely eliminated in Spanish!

Try this: Treat the verbs in the "AR" family as you would "to speak" or "hablar." End the verb with an "o" when you're talking about yourself; "hablo" or "I speak". Change the verb ending from an "o" to an "a" for "habla" or "you speak." Use this form when you're talking to someone else.

English	Español	Guide
I need	Necesito	nay-say-SEE-toe
You need	Necesita	nay-say-SEE-ta

The Sweet 16 Verbs

The "sweet 16 verbs" are some of the most common, regular verbs you will use when you begin speaking Spanish. They are indispensible communication tools. Many of them are *cognates* or words that closely resemble their English equivalents. Their close relationship to English makes them even easier to remember—and to use! Even if you are unable to remember how to change the letters on the end of the verb to conjugate it correctly, use the basic, unconjugated form as you see in the table on page 32. Wheather you conjugate it or not, the single verb alone carries all the meaning!

31

English	Español	Guide
To accept	Aceptar	ah-sep-TAR
To ask	Preguntar	prey-goon-TAR
To baptize	Bautizar	bow-t-CZAR
To call	Llamar	ya-MAR
To carry	Llevar	yea-VAR
To help	Ayudar	eye-you-DAR
To lift	Levantar	lay-van-TAR
To need	Necesitar	nay-say-see-TAR
To pray	Rezar	ray-CZAR
To preach	Predicar	pray-d-CAR
To prepare	Preparar	pray-pa-RAR
To return	Regresar	ray-grey-SAR
To sing	Cantar	can-TAR
To use	Usar	oo-SAR
To work	Trabajar	tra-baa-HAR
To worship	Adorar	ah-door-RAR

**Note: To make a sentence negative, say no in front of the verb.

Example: I don't need.	**No necesito.**
You don't need	**No necesita.**

Irregular Verbs: The Big Five

Now that you have had the opportunity to learn about the tremendous number of verbs that follow regular patterns in Spanish, it's time to take a look at others that don't follow the rules. They are unpredictable, but they are very important. In fact, they reflect some of man's oldest concepts. That's why they tend to be irregular. These words were in use long before language rules and patterns were set. There are two verbs in Spanish that mean "to be." The others are: "to have," "to make" and "to go." Because they don't follow the rules, you will need to memorize them. However, that should be easy because you will use and hear them often.

In English, the "to be" verb is "I am," "you are," "he is" etc. The Spanish version is **ser** and **estar**. *Ser* is used to express permanent things such as your nationality or profession. *Estar* is used when talking about location or conditions that change such as a person's health.

	Ser			**Estar**	
Yo **soy**	Nosotros **somos**		Yo **estoy**	Nosotros **estamos**	
Tú **eres**			Tú **estás**		
Él **es**	Ellos **son**		Él **está**	Ellos **están**	
Ella **es**	Ellas **son**		Ella **está**	Ellas **están**	
Usted **es**	Uds. **son**		Usted **está**	Uds. **están**	

The verb *"to have"* in Spanish, is *muy importante*. In English, we say that we are hot, cold, hungry, thirsty, right, wrong or sleepy, but in Spanish, these are conditions that you have. Some of the expressions mean something totally different than expected if you confuse the verbs, so be careful!

Tener	
Yo **tengo**	Nosotros **tenemos**
Tú **tienes**	
Él **tiene**	Ellos **tienen**
Ella **tiene**	Ellas **tienen**
Usted **tiene**	Ustedes **tienen**

In Spanish, the verb that means *"to do"* also means *"to make."* It's not unusual for one verb to have multiple meanings. There are many expressions that require the use of this verb, but you will use it most when you talk about the weather. That's a safe subject and one that everyone worldwide discusses! **¿Qué tiempo hace?** What's the weather? **Hace frío.** (It's cold.) **Hace sol.** (It's sunny). **Hace calor.** (It's hot) **Hace viento** (It's windy.). Here are two exceptions: **Está lloviendo.** (It's raining.) and **Está nevando.** (It's snowing.)

Hacer

Yo **hago**	Nosotros **hacemos**
Tú **haces**	
Él **hace**	Ellos **hacen**
Ella **hace**	Ellas **hacen**
Usted **hace**	Ustedes **hacen.**

The last of the big five is perhaps the easiest to use. It's the verb that means, *"to go"*. In Spanish, the verb is *ir* which is pronounced like the English word "ear." *In* both English and Spanish, we use parts of the word to make the future tense or to talk about things that we are going to do. Look at the parts of *ir*. Now look back at the parts of the verb *ser*. Do you notice any similarities?

Ir

Yo **voy**	Nosotros **vamos**
Tú **vas**	
Él **va**	Ellos **van**
Ella **va**	Ellas **van**
Usted **va**	Ustedes **van**

When you want to say something that you are going to do, start with "I'm going" or *voy*.

Next, insert the word "*a*" and the basic verb that states what it is that you're going to do. Try it! It's easy.

Voy a visitar a mi familia.
I am going to visit my family.

Mario va a comprar la medicina.
Mario is going to buy the medicine.

**Note: The whole concept of irregular verbs can be quite daunting. Don't let it defeat you! We have many irregular verbs in English. Every language has them. The only way to master them is to use them. Make them your own! Try writing different parts of a verb on your desk calendar. That way, the words will be right in front of you every time you look down. When you see a word, say it to yourself. You will have it conquered in no time.

Idioms: Using the Right Verb at the Right Time

Using the right verb at the right time is very important in some very common Spanish phrases. In some of these phrases using the wrong verb can change the meaning of what you are trying to say.
The following phrases require the use of *tener* which means *to have.* In English we use a form of the verb "to be."

These are phrases you must learn, even though the translation will feel may feel odd to you. Phrases like these are called *idiomatic expressions.* Learning them is extremely important to basic conversational skills.

35

TENER: To have   **Tengo:** I have   **Tiene:** You have

English	Español	Guide
Hot	Calor	ca-**LORE**
Hungry	Hambre	**AM**-bray
Cold	Frío.	**FREE**-oh
Ashamed	Vergüenza	ver-goo-**N**-sa
In pain.	Dolor	doe-**LORE**
Afraid of	Miedo de	me-**A**-doe day
Right	Razón	rah-**SEWN**
Thirsty	Sed	said
Sleepy	Sueño	soo-**WAYNE**-nyo
xx years old	*xx* años	xx **AHN**-nyos

Tips & Tidbits
It is important to use the correct verb in these common expressions. Using the wrong verb can change the meaning of what you are trying to say!

What's the Weather? — ¿Qué tiempo hace?

A general topic for discussion in any culture is always the weather. Discussing the weather in Spanish requires a different verb from the one used in English. If you say to your host, "*Está frío,*" he or she would think that you were talking about something you had touched. In Spanish, use the verb **hacer** which means "to do" or "to make" to describe the weather. This verb is one of the big five irregulars.

36

English	Español	Guide
To be nice weather	Hace buen tiempo	AH-say boo-WAYNE t-M-po
To be hot	Hace calor	AH-say ca-LORE
To be cool	Hace fresco	AH-say FRES-co
To be sunny	Hace sol	AH-say sol
To be windy	Hace viento	AH-say v-N-toe
To be cold	Hace frío	AH-say FREE-oh
Rain	Lluvia	U-v-ah
To rain	Llover	YO-ver
What's the weather?	¿Qué tiempo hace?	kay t-M-poe AH-say

Tips & Tidbits

1. Latin American countries use the Celsius scale for measuring temperature. What's the difference? Here's a simple example: 0 degrees Celsius equals 32 degrees Fahrenheit.

2. Use the internet to research the weather conditions in the country where your mission trip will take place. The up-to-date information will help you know what to pack.

Special Uses of Ser and Estar

The verbs *ser* and *estar* both mean the same thing in English: *to be,* but **how can two verbs mean the same thing?** It's because *ser* and *estar* are used in very different ways. Spanish sees these two verbs differently and uses them in very precise ways. Listed below are some simple guidelines on their usage:

Common Uses of Ser

To express an permanent quality or characteristic

La puerta es de madera.   The door is made of wood.

El hospital es enorme.   The hospital is enormous.

Los doctores son importantes. Doctors are important.

To describe or identify

Mi amigo es médico.   My friend is a doctor.

El estudiante es alto.   The student is tall.

To indicate nationality or profession

Pedro es mexicano.   Pedro is Mexican.

Soy de Carolina del Norte.   I'm from North Carolina.

Soy maestra.   I'm a teacher.

To express ownership

Este es mi auto.   This is my car.

Este es mi Biblia.   This is my Bible.

To express time and dates

¿Qué hora es?   What time is it?

Hoy es el nueve de junio.   Today is the 9th of June.

With impersonal expressions.

Es importante estudiar.   It's important to study.

Es necesario leer.   It's necessary to read.

Tips and Tidbits

In general conversation, the most common parts of the verb ser that are used are "soy" or I am and "es" which means you are. Can you think of examples where these two forms will come in handy on your mission trip?

Common Uses of Estar

To express location

Estoy en la oficina.	I am in the office.
San José está en Costa Rica.	San José is in Costa Rica.
¿Dónde está la iglesia?	Where is the church?

To indicate someone's health

Mi esposa está enferma.	My wife is sick.
¿Cómo está usted?	How are you?
Estoy cansada.	I'm tired.

Estar is also used as a helping verb

Estoy hablando.	I am speaking.
Carmen está trabajando.	Carmen is working.
Ella está cantando.	She is singing.

Tips & Tidbits

Don't let your concerns about using the correct verb for "to be" keep you from talking! This concept in Spanish is tough for everyone. Native speakers will help you!

Notice from the examples that *ser* is used more frequently than *estar*. Even though the usage of *ser* and *estar* seems complicated in the beginning, both verbs are used so frequently in conversation that you will quickly become comfortable using them. In most cases, you will be understood, even if you use the wrong one.

By the Numbers

Spanish speakers tend to say numbers extremely fast! Don't hesitate to ask for numbers to be repeated more slowly. If you don't remember those phrases, review *Spanish Sounds Rápido—What Do I Do Now?*

Number	Español	Guide
0	Cero	SAY-row
1	Uno	OO-no
2	Dos	dose
3	Tres	trays
4	Cuatro	coo-AH-trow
5	Cinco	SINK-oh
6	Seis	SAY-ees
7	Siete	see-A-tay
8	Ocho	OH-cho
9	Nueve	new-A-vay
10	Diez	d-ACE
11	Once	ON-say
12	Doce	DOSE-a
13	Trece	TRAY-say
14	Catorce	ca-TOR-say
15	Quince	KEEN-say
16	Diez y seis	d-ACE e SAY-ees
17	Diez y siete	d-ACE e see-ATE-tay
10	Dien y ssho	d-ACE e OH-cho
19	Diez y nueve	d-ACE e new-A-vay
20	Veinte	VAIN-tay
21	Veinte y uno	VAIN-tay e OO-no

Number	Español	Guide
22	Veinte y dos	VAIN-tay e dose
23	Veinte y tres	VAIN-tay e trays
24	Veinte y cuatro	VAIN-tay e coo-AH-trow
25	Veinte y cinco	VAIN-tay e SINK-oh
26	Veinte y seis	VAIN-tay e SAY-ees
27	Veinte y siete	VAIN-tay e see-A-tay
28	Veinte y ocho	VAIN-tay e OH-cho -
29	Veinte y nueve	VAIN-tay e new-A-vay
30	Treinta	TRAIN-ta
40	Cuarenta	kwah-RAIN-ta
50	Cincuenta	seen-KWAIN-ta
60	Sesenta	say-SAIN-ta
70	Setenta	say-TAIN-ta
80	Ochenta	oh-CHAIN-ta
90	Noventa	no-VAIN-ta
100	Cien	see-IN
200	Doscientos	dose-see-N-toes
300	Trescientos	tray-see-N-toes
400	Cuatrocientos	coo-AH-troh-see-N-toes
500	Quinientos	keen-e-N-toes
600	Seiscientos	SAY-ees-see-N-toes
700	Setecientos	SAY-tay-see-N-toes
800	Ochocientos	OH-choh- see-N-toes
900	Novecientos	NO-vay-see-N-toes
1,000	Mil	meal

Days of the Week and Months of the Year

Los Días de la Semana

English	Español	Guide
Monday	**lunes**	LOON-ace
Tuesday	martes	MAR-tays
Wednesday	**miércoles**	me-AIR-co-lace
Thursday	jueves	who-WAVE-ace
Friday	viernes	v-AIR-nace
Saturday	sábado	SAH-ba-doe
Sunday	domingo	doe-MING-go

Use this format to give dates: *El (date) de (month).*

Los Meses del Año

English	Español	Guide
January	enero	n-NAY-row
February	febrero	fay-BRAY-row
March	marzo	MAR-so
April	abril	ah-BRILL
May	mayo	MY-oh
June	junio	WHO-knee-oh
July	julio	WHO-lee-oh
August	agosto	ah-GOSE-toe
September	septiembre	sep-tee-EM-bray
October	octubre	oc-TOO-bray
November	noviembre	no-v-EM-bray
December	diciembre	d-see-EM-bray

What Time Is It? — ¿Qué Hora Es?

The concept of time is something that varies from culture to culture. Many countries place less emphasis on being on time for certain things than Americans. In Latino culture, most people live for the present. It can be especially true in one's personal life; however, on the job, everyone knows the value of *puntualidad*. *¡Es muy importante!*

Learning to tell time is another good way to put your Spanish numbers to good use

¿Qué hora es? means *what time is it?*

It's one o'clock.	Es la una.
It's two o'clock.	Son las dos.
It's 3:30.	Son las tres y media.
It's 5:45.	Son las seis menos quince.

Use the phrases *de la mañana* to indicate morning, and *de la tarde* to indicate afternoon. In addition, midnight is *medianoche* and noon is *mediodía*.

To find out at what time something takes place, ask: *¿A qué hora...?*

¿A qué hora es la reunión?	What time is the meeting?
¿A qué hora termina?	What time do you finish?

The Questions Everyone Should Know

English	Español	Guide
Who?	¿Quién?	key-N
What?	¿Qué?	kay
Which?	¿Cuál?	coo-ALL
When?	¿Cuándo?	KWAN-doe
Where?	¿Dónde?	DON-day
Why?	¿Por qué?	pour KAY
How?	¿Cómo?	CO-mo
What's happening?	¿Qué pasa?	kay PA-sa
How much?	¿Cuánto?	KWAN-toe
How many?	¿Cuántos?	KWAN-toes

When you ask a question in Spanish, it will take on the same form as a question in English. Start with the question word that asks the information you need. Follow the question word with a verb, and give your voice an upward inflection.

In Spanish, you can also make a question by ending your sentence with ¿no? Here's an example: *Cancún está en México, ¿no?* When you end a sentence with "no" like this, it takes on the meaning of "isn't it."

How are you?   ¿Cómo está?
How much does it cost?   ¿Cuánto cuesta?
Where are you from?   ¿De dónde es?

Getting the Información

Listed below are common phrases that are used to fill out almost any questionnaire. It seems like most forms ask for much of the same information in almost the same order. By learning a few simple phrases, you can use this format to your advantage.

There are so many times when we need to ask for very basic information. Most of these questions begin with the words *"what is your."* When you are asking this type of question, remember that it's not always necessary to form a complete sentence to have good communication. The information you are asking for is much more important than the phrase "what is your"? As long as you remember to make what you say *sound* like a question by giving your voice an *upward* inflection, people will interpret what you've said *as* a question.

Use the form on the following page; it asks for very basic information. To help you practice, work with a partner. Make up new information about yourself and complete the form. At each practice session, one of you will ask the questions and the other will provide the answers to fill in the information requested. This is a great practice exercise — most of the time the questions you ask will be the same, but the answers you receive will always be different!

What's your. . .	**¿Cuál es su. . .**
	coo-ALL es sue

English	Español	Guide
Full name	Nombre completo	NOM-bray com-PLAY-toe
First name	Primer nombre	pre-MARE NOM-bray
Middle name	Segundo nombre	say-GOON-doe NOM-bray
Last name (surname)	Apellido	ah-pay-YE-doe
Paternal surname	Apellido paterno	ah-pay-YE-doe pa-TER-no
Maternal surname	Apellido materno	ah-pay-YE-doe ma-TER-no
Address	Dirección	d-wreck-see-ON
Age	Edad	a-DAD
Date of birth	Fecha de nacimiento	FAY-cha day na-see-me-N-toe
Nationality	Nacionalidad	na-see-on-nal-e-DAD
Place of birth	Lugar de nacimiento	loo-GAR day na-see-me-N-toe
Home telephone number	Número de teléfono de su casa	NEW-may-row day tay-LAY-fo-no day sue CA-sa
Name of husband/wife	Nombre de esposo (a)	NOM-bray day es-PO-so (sah)
Name of child	Nombre de niño	NOM-bray day KEEN-yo

46

Words for Worship

Going on a mission trip will give you unforgettable opportunities to worship. The memories of the services you attend may be the greatest blessings of your journey. The words in this vocabulary list will help you praise God anywhere in Latin America that your mission trip takes you.

English	Español	Guide
Bible	Biblia	B-blee-ah
Blasphemy	Blasfemia	blahs-**FAY**-me-ah
Blessing	Bendición	ben-d-see-**ON**
Blood	Sangre	**SAHN**-gray
Body	Cuerpo	coo-**WEAR**-po
Cassock	Sotana	so-**TA**-na
Cathedral	Catedral	ca-tay-**DRAL**
Chalice	Cáliz	**CA**-lease
Chapter	Capítulo	ca-**P**-to-low
Charity	Caridad	ca-ree-**DAHD**
Confession	Confesión	con-fes-see-**ON**
Confirmation	Confirmación	con-fear-ma-c-**ON**
Congregation	Fieles	fee-**EH**-lace
Consecrated wafer	Hostia	ohs-**T**-ah
Convent	Convento	con-**VEN**-toe
Cross	Cruz	cruise
Devil	Diablo	d-**AH**-blow
Eternal	Eterno	eh-**TER**-no

English	Español	Guide
First communion	Primera comunión	pre-MAY-rah co-moo-knee-ON
Forever	Siempre	see-M-pray
God	Díos	D-os
	Señor	sen-YOUR
God bless you.	Díos te bendiga	D-os tay ben-D-ga
Gospel	Evangelio	eh-van-HEL-e-oh
Halo	Aureola	ow-ray-OH-la
Heart	Corazón	core-rah-SEWN
Heaven	Cielo	see-A-low
Hell	Infierno	een-fee-AIR-no
Heresy	Herejía	eh-ray-HE-ah
Heretic	Hereje	eh-RAY-hey
Holiness	Santidad	san-t-DAHD
Holy Spirit	Espíritu Santo	es-P-ree-to SAN-toe
Holy Water	Agua bendito	AH-goo-ah ben-D-toe
Incense	Incienso	een-see-N-so
Jesus	Jesús	hey-ZEUS
Christ	Cristo	CREASE-toe
Leader	Líder	LEE-dare
Love	Amor	ah-MORE
Mass	Misa	ME-sa
Miracle	Milagro	me-LA-grow

English	Español	Guide
Mission trip	Viaje de misión	v-AH-hey day me-see-ON
Monastery	Monasterio	mo-nas-TAY-ree-oh
Non-believer	Pagano	pa-GAH-no
Offering	Oferta	oh-FAIR-ta
Parable	Parábola	pa-RAH-bo-la
Parish	Parroquia	pa-ROW-kee-ah
Piety	Piedad	p-eh-DAHD
Pious	Piadoso	p-ah-DOE-so
Prayer	Oración	oh-rah-see-ON
Psalm	Salmo	SAL-mo
Rosary	Rosario	row-SA-ree-oh
Sermon	Sermón	ser-MON
Service	Servicio	ser-V-see-oh
Sin	Pecado	pay-CA-doe
Theology	Teología	tay-oh-low-HE-ah
To baptize	Bautizar	bow-t-CZAR
To kneel	Arrodillarse	ah-row-d-YAR-say
To pray	Rezar	ray-CZAR
To preach	Predicar	pray-D-car
Verse	Verso	VER-so
Vestments	Vestiduras	ves-t-DO-rahs
Vows	Promesas solemnes	pro-MAY-sas so-LIMB-nes
Worship	Adorar	ah-doe-RAHR

Within the Church

When I travel abroad, taking part in worship services adds an extra dimension of depth to my trip, even if I don't understand the language. Seeing different works of art, hearing indiginous music and experiencing the power of God is always a powerful and moving experience. Here is a list containing areas within the church. If your mission trip takes you inside of a church, how many of these areas can you name?

English	Español	Guide
Aisle	Nave lateral	NA-vay la-teh-**RAL**
Altar	Altar	ahl-**TAR**
Apse	Ábside	**AB**-see-day
Baptismal font	Pila bautismal	**P**-la bow-tees-**MAL**
Ceiling	Techo	**TAY**-cho
Choir Loft	Coro	**CO**-row
Chapel	Capilla	ca-**P**-ya
Floor	Piso	**P**-so
Font	Pila	**P**-la
Foundation	Fundación	foon-da-see-**ON**
Hymn book	Himnario	em-**NAR**-ree-oh
Lectern	Atril	ah **TREEL**
Nave	Nave	**NA**-vay
Pew	Banco	**BAN**-co
Pulpit	Púlpito	**POOL**-p-toe

English	Español	Guide
Sanctuary	Santuario	sahn-to-ARE-ree-oh
Stained glass	Vidriera	V-dre-EH-rah
Steeple	Campanario	cam-pa-NA-ree-oh
Transept	Crucero	crew-SAY-row
Vestibule	Minister	ves-T-boo-low
Wall	Pared	pa-RED
Window	Ventana	ven-TA-na
Vestry	Sacristía	sa-crees-T-ah

Musical Instruments

Making a joyful noice with music is so important to worship. The kinds of instruments used in your home church for worship may be extremely different from the ones used in your Latin American mission church. In addition to the instruments listed below, ask you hosts about indiginous instruments that are only found in the country you visit. See if you can purchase one in the local market to take home. It will make a great souvenir of your journey.

English	Español	Guide
Bell	Campana	cam-PA-na
Carol	Villancico	v-yahn-SEE-co
Choir	Coro	CO-row
Cymbals	Platillos	plah-T-yos
Drum	Tambor	tam-BORE

English	Español	Guide
Flute	Flauta	flah-OO-ta
Guitar	Guitarra	gee-TAR-rah
Harp	Harpa	ARE-pa
Organ	Órgano	OR-gah-no
Piano	Piano	p-AH-no
Song	Canción	can-see-ON
Trumpet	Trompeta	trom-PEH-ta
Voice	Voz	vohs

People in the Church

English	Español	Guide
Apostle	Apóstol	ah-POS-tol
Archbishop	Arzobispo	are-so-BEES-po
Bishop	Obispo	oh-BEES-po
Bride	Novia	NO-v-ah
Bridesmaid	Dama de honor	DA-ma day on-NOR
Chaplain	Capellán	ca-pay-YAN
Choir director	Director del coro	d-wreck-TOR de CORE-row
Deacon	Diácono	d-AH-co-no
Disciple	Discípulo	dees-SEE-poo-low
Evangelist	Evangelista	eh-vahn-hey-LEES-ta
Groom	Novio	NO-v-oh

English	Español	Guide
Minister	Ministro	me-KNEE-strow
Monk	Monje	MON-hey
Nun	Monja	MON-ha
Pastor	Pastor *(a)*	pas-TOR
Pilgrim	Peregrino	peh-ray-GREE-no
Pope	Papa	PA-pa
Priest	Cura	COO-rah
Saint	Santo	SAHN-toe
	Santa	SAHN-ta

Books of the Bible

Old Testament **Antiguo Testamento**

English	Español	Guide
Genesis	Génesis	HEY-nay-sees
Exodus	Éxodo	EX-oh-doe
Leviticus	Levítico	lay-V-tee-co
Numbers	Números	NEW-may-rows
Deuteronomy	Deuteronomio	day-oo-ter-oh-no-ME-oh
Joshua	Josué	ho-sue-EH
Judges	Jueces	who-EH-sehs
Ruth	Rut	root
1st Samuel	Primero Samuel	pre-MAY-row sa-moo-L

English	Español	Guide
2nd Samuel	Segundo Samuel	say-GOON-doe sa-moo-L
1st Kings	Primero Reyes	pre-MAY-row RAY-ace
2nd Kings	Segundo Reyes	say-GOON-doe RAY-ace
1st Chronicles	Primero Crónicas	pre-MAY-row CROW-knee-cas
2nd Chronicles	Segundo Crónicas	say-GOON-doe CROW-knee-cas
Ezra	Esdras	EHS-drahs
Nehemiah	Nehemías	nay-eh-ME-ahs
Esther	Ester	ehs-TER
Job	Job	hob
Psalms	Salmos	SAL-mos
Proverbs	Proverbios	pro-VER-b-ohs
Ecclesiastes	Eclesiastés	eh-cleh-see-ahs-TAYS
Song of Solomon	Cantares	can-TAR-ace
Isaiah	Isaías	e-sa-E-ahs
Jeremiah	Jeremías	hey-ray-ME-ahs
Lamentations	Lamentaciones	la-men-ta-see-OH-ace
Ezekiel	Ezequiel	eh-say-key-L
Daniel	Daniel	dah-knee-L
Hosea	Oseas	oh-SAY-ahs
Amos	Amós	ah-MOS
Obadiah	Abdías	ahb-D-ahs

English	Español	Guide
Jonah	Jonás	ho-NAS
Micah	Miqueas	me-KAY-ahs
Nahum	Nahúm	na-OOM
Habakkuk	Habacuc	ah-ba-COOK
Zephaniah	Sofonías	so-fo-KNEE-ahs
Haggai	Hageo	ah-HEY-oh
Zechariah	Zacarías	sa-ca-REE-ahs
Malachi	Malaquías	ma-la-KEY-ahs

New Testament   Nuevo Testamento

English	Español	Guide
Matthew	Mateo	ma-TAY-oh
Mark	Marcos	MAR-cos
Luke	Lucas	LOO-cas
John	Juan	wan
Acts	Hechos	EH-chos
Romans	Romanos	ro-MAN-nos
1st Corinthians	1 Corintios	pre-MAY-row co-REEN-t-ohs
2nd Corinthians	2 Corintios	say-GOON-doe co-REEN-t-ohs
Galatians	Gálatas	GA-la-tahs
Ephesians	Efesios	eh-FAY-see-ohs

English	Español	Guide
Philippians	Filipenses	fee-lee-**PEN**-sehs
Colossians	Colosenses	co-lo-**SEN**-sehs
1st Tessalonians	1 Tesalonicenses	pre-**MAY**-row tes-sa-low-knee-**SEN**-ces
2nd Tessalonians	2 Tesalonicenses	say-**GOON**-doe tes-sa-low-knee-**SEN**-ces
1st Timothy	1 Timoteo	pre-**MAY**-row t-mo-**TAY**-oh
2nd Timothy	2 Timoteo	say-**GOON**-doe t-mo-**TAY**-oh
Titus	Tito	**TEE**-toe
Philemon	Filemón	fee-lay-**MON**
Hebrews	Hebreos	eh-**BRAY**-os
James	Santiago	san-t-**AH**-go
1st Peter	1 Pedro	pre-**MAY**-row **PAY**-drow
2nd Peter	2 Pedro	say-**GOON**-doe **PAY**-drow
1st John	1 Juan	pre-**MAY**-row wan
2nd John	2 Juan	say-**GOON**-doe wan
3rd John	3 Juan	ter-**SAY**-row wan
Jude	Judas	**WHO**-das
Revelations	Apocalipsis	ah-po-ca-**LEAP**-sus

Favorite Bible Verses

As you prepare for your mission trip, think about your favorite Bible verses and make translations of them. These will get you started.

I am with you and will watch over you wherever you go.
Genesis 28:15

Estoy contigo. Te protegeré por dondequiera que vayas.
Génesis 28:15

The Lord is with me; I will not be afraid.   Psalm 118:6
Dios está conmigo; no tendré miedo.   Salmos 118:6

Your word is a lamp unto my feet and a light for my path.
Psalm 119:105

Tu palabra es una lámpara a mis pies y luz para mi camino.
Salmos 119:105

I will instruct you, I will show you the way you must to go, I will give you counsel, and I will watch over you. Psalm 32:8

Yo te instruiré, yo te mostraré el camino que debes seguir, yo te daré consejos y velaré por ti.   Salmos 32:8

Your kingdom is everlasting; thy dominion endures through all generations. The Lord is faithful to his Word and holy in all his works. Psalm 145:13

Tu reino es un reino eterno; tu dominio permanece por todas las edades. Fiel es el Señor a su palabra y bondadoso en todas sus obras. Salmos 145:13

The Lord's Prayer

Padre nuestro, que estás en los cielos,
santificado sea tu nombre.
venga tu reino.
hágase tu voluntad, como en el cielo,
así también en la tierra.
El pan nuestro de cada día, dánoslo hoy.
y perdónanos nuestras deudas,
como también nosotros perdonamos a nuestros deudores.
Y no nos metas en tentación,
mas líbranos del mal;
porque tuyo es el reino, y el poder, y la gloria,
por todos los siglos.
Amén.

Psalm 23

Jehovah es mi pastor; nada me faltará.
En prados de tiernos pastos me hace descansar.
Junto a aguas tranquilas me conduce.
Confortará mi alma
Me guiará por sendas de justicia por amor de su nombre.
Aunque ande en valle de sombra de muerte,
no temeré mal alguno, porque Tú estarás conmigo.
Tu vara y tu cayado me infundirán aliento.
Preparas mesa delante de Mí en presencia de mis adversarios.
Unges mi cabeza con aceite; mi copa Está rebosando.
Ciertamente el bien y la misericordia me seguirán
todos los Días de mi vida,
y en la casa de Jehovah moraré por Días sin fin.

Canciones Favoritos

Jesus Loves Me

Jesus love me, this I know,
For the Bible tells me so.
Little ones to Him belong,
They are weak, but
He is strong.

Yes, Jesus loves me (x 3)
The Bible tells me so.

Jesus loves me, He who died
Heaven's gate to open wide,
He will wash away my sin,
Let His little child come in.

Cristo Me Ama

Cristo me ama, bien lo sé,
Su palabra me hace ver,
Que los niños son de aquel
Quien es nuestro amigo fiel.

Cristo me ama (x3)
La Biblia dice así.

Cristo me ama, pues murió,
Y el cielo me abrió.
Él mis culpas quitará,
Y la entrada me dará.

Amazing Grace

Twas grace that taught
my heart to fear,
And grace my fears relieved.
How precious did that
grace appear,
The hour I first believed.

When we've been there
ten thousand years,
Bright shining as the sun,
We've no less days to sing
God's praise, than when
we'd first begun.

Sublime Gracia

Sublime gracia
del Señor
Que un infeliz salvó.
Fui ciego más hoy miro yo
Perdido y
Él me halló.

Su gracia me enseñó
a temer,
Mis dudas ahuyentó.
¡Oh, cuán precioso fue
a mi ser
Al dar mi corazón!

What a Friend We Have in Jesus

What a friend
we have in Jesus,
All our sins and griefs
to bear,
What a privilege to carry,
Everything to God
in prayer.
Oh, what peace
we often forfeit,
Oh, what needless pain
we bear,
All because we do not carry
Everything to God,
in prayer.

Have we trials and
temptations?
Is there trouble anywhere?
We should never be
discouraged. Take it to the
Lord in prayer.
Can we find a friend
so faithful who will all our
sorrows share?
Jesus knows our every
weakness. Take it to the
Lord in prayer.

Qué Amigo Nos Es Cristo

¡Oh, qué amigo
nos es Cristo!
Él llevó nuestro dolor,
Y nos manda que llevemos,
Todo A Dios en oración.

¿Vive el hombre desprovisto
De paz, gozo y santo amor?
Esto es porque no llevamos,
Todo a Dios en oración.

¿Vives débil y cargado
De cuidados y temor?

A Jesús, refugio eterno,
Dile todo en oración.

¿Te desprecian tus amigos?
Cuéntaselo en oración.
En sus brazos de amor
tierno, paz tendrá
tu corazón.

Talking to Children

Talking to the children you meet on your mission trip will be one of the most rewarding parts of your journey. Children are naturally curious, learn languages quickly and will be eager to share their language and culture with you. Things you like and things you dislike make good topics of conversation. The following is a list of toys, games and places that will help you get started building relationships with the children in your mission community.

I like = Me gusta or me gustan (pl.)
I don't like = No me gusta
Do you like = ¿Te gusta or te gustan (pl.)

English	Español	Guide
What's your name?	¿Cómo te llamas?	CO-mo te YA-mas
How old are you?	¿Cuántos años tienes?	coo-WAN-toes AHN-yos t-N-ace
Do you have any brothers and sisters?	¿Tienes hermanos o hermanas?	t-N-ace air-MA-nose oh air-MAHN-nas
Tell me.	Dime.	D-may
Come here.	Ven aquí.	ven ah-KEY
Where do you live?	¿Dónde vives?	DON-day V-vase
What is your mother's name?	¿Cómo se llama tu madre?	CO-mo say YA-ma to MA-dray
What is your father's name?	¿Cómo se llama tu padre?	CO-mo say YA-ma to PA-dray
Do you like....?	¿Te gusta....?	tay GOO-sta

English	Español	Guide
Animal	Animale	ah-nay-**MAL**
Balloons	Globos	**GLOW**-bows
Bird	Pájaro	**PA**-ha-row
Blocks	Bloques de madera	**BLOW**-kays day ma-**DARE**-rah
Book	Libro	**LEE**-bro
Cards	Cartas	**CAR**-tas
Cat	Gato	**GA**-toe
Checkers	Juego de damas	who-**WAY**-go day **DA**-mas
Chewing gum	Chicle	**CHEEK**-lay
Chocolate	Chocolate	cho-co-**LA**-tay
Coloring/painting	Pintar	peen-**TAR**
Crayons	Gises *(Chaulk – Mex)* Lápices de color	**HE**-sace **LA**-p-ace day co-**LORE**
Dog	Perro	pay-**ROW**
Doll	Muñeca	moon-**YECK**-ah
Drawing *(v)*	Dibujando	d-boo-**HAHN**-doe
Fish	Pez	pez
Flowers	Flores	**FLOOR**-rays
Games	Juegos	who-**WAY**-gos
Horse	Caballo	ca-**BUY**-yo
Jokes	Chistes	**CHI**-stays
Jump rope	Cuerda para brincar	coo-**AIR**-da **PA**-rah breen-**CAR**
Music	Música	**MOO**-see-ca

English	Español	Guide
Parties	Fiestas	fee-ES-tas
Playing music	Tocando música	toe-CAHN-doe MOO-see-ca
Puzzles	Rompecabezas	rowm-pay-ca-BAY-sas
Reading	Leyendo	lay-N-doe
School	Escuela	es-coo-WAY-la
Songs	Canciones	can-see-ON-ace
Sports	Deportes	day-POR-tays
Stories	Cuentos	coo-WAYNE-toes
Stuffed animals	Animales de peluche	ah-nay-MAL-ace day pay-LOO-chay
Beach	Playa	la PLY-ya
Jungle	Selva	la SELL-va
Mountains	Montañas	mon-TAHN-yas
To play	Jugar	who-GAR
Toys	Juguetes	who-GET-tays
Turtle	Tortuga	tor-TOO-gas
Writing	Escribiendo	es-scree-b-N-doe
You are	Eres	EH-rays
Adorable	Adorable	ah-door-RAH-blays
Angel	Ángel	AHN-hel
Cute	Mono	MO-no
Funny	Chistoso	chees-TOE-so
Handsome	Guapo	goo-WA-po
Nice	Simpático	seem-PA-t-co

63

English	Español	Guide
Precious	Precioso	pray-see-**OH**-so
Pretty	Bonita	bow-**KNEE**-ta
Shy	Tímido	T-me-doe

The Family — La Familia

For Latinos nothing is more important than their families. The family group is always more important than the individual. No sacrifice is too great if it helps the family.

Children are considered precious gifts. Wives, mothers and grandmothers are highly respected. Remember that the maternal side of the family is so important that traditional Hispanics carry their mother's surname or *materno apellido* as a part of their complete name. You are certainly going to hear about members of the family from your mission trip hosts. This topic is something all of us like to talk about!

English	Español	Guide
Aunt	Tía	**TEE**-ah
Uncle	Tío	**TEE**-oh
Brother	Hermano	air-**MAN**-oh
Sister	Hermana	air-**MAN**-ah
Brother-in-law	Cuñado	coon-**YA**-doe
Sister-in-law	Cuñada	coon-**YA**-da
Child	Niño *(a)*	**KEEN**-yo

English	Español	Guide
Cousin	Primo *(a)*	PRE-mo
Daughter	Hija	E-ha
Son	Hijo	E-ho
Daughter-in-law	Nuera	new-**AIR**-rah
Son-in-law	Yerno	**YEAIR**-no
Father	Padre	**PA**-dray
Mother	Madre	**MA**-dray
Father-in-law	Suegro	soo-**A**-grow
Mother-in-law	Suegra	soo-**A**-gra
Granddaughter	Nieta	knee-**A**-tah
Grandson	Nieto	knee-**A**-toe
Grandfather	Abuelo	ah-boo-**A**-low
Grandmother	Abuela	ah-boo-**A**-la
Husband	Esposo	es-**PO**-so
Wife	Esposa	es-**POE**-sa
Godfather	Padrino	pa-**DREE**-no
Godmother	Madrina	ma-**DREE**-no
Goddaughter	Ahijada	ah-e-**HA**-da
Godson	Ahijado	ah-e-**HA**-doe

Tips and Tidbits:
Before leaving for your trip, take the words and phrases found in this section on the family and begin writing a self-description. Everyone will want to know about your family in the USA.

Accentuate the Positive

Showing enthusiasm for your mission trip hosts and the work you are doing will make for a highly memorable trip. Use these phrases to give everyone positive feedback and watch smiles begin to light up their faces.

English	Español	Guide
It's…!	¡Es…!	es
Excellent	Excelente	x-see-**LEN**-tay
Fantastic	Fantástico	fan-**TAS**-t-co
Good	Bueno	boo-**WAY**-no
Very good!	¡Muy bien!	mooy BN
Very important!	Muy importante!	mooy m-por-**TAN**-tay
I respect you.	Le respeto.	lay race-**PAY**-toe

Giving Directions

The ability to give directions in *español* is one of the most practical skills you can have. Giving directions will be a *grande* plus to your conversational ability. Slowly, you can start to learn this vocabulary by knowing simple things, such as the four directions: north, south, east and west. Then, add turns like right and left. Before you know it, you'll be able to give directions to almost any place in town.

English	Español	Guide
Where is…?	¿Dónde está…?	DON-day es-TA
Above	Encima	n-SEE-ma
Aisle	Pasillo	pa-SEE-yo
Avenue	Avenida	ah-ven-KNEE-da
Behind	Detrás	day-TRAHS
Beside	Al lado de	al LA-doe day
Down	Abajo	ah-BAA-ho
East	Este	ES-tay
Far	Lejos	LAY-hos
Here	Aquí	ah-KEY
In front of	En frente de	n FREN-tay day
Inside	Adentro	ah-DEN-tro
Near	Cerca de	CER-ca day
North	Norte	NOR-tay
Outside	Afuera	ah-foo-AIR-ah
Over there	Allá	ah-YA
South	Sur	SUE-er
Straight ahead	Adelante	ah-day-LAN-tay
Street	Calle	ca-YEA
There	Allí	ah-YE
To the left	A la izquierda	ah la ees-key-AIR-dah
To the right	A la derecha	ah la day-RAY-cha
Turn	Doble	DOE-blay
Up	Arriba	ah-REE-ba
West	Oeste	oh-ES-tay

Around Town

Common places around town can provide you with great practice opportunities. The next time you go out to run errands, check the list below. Where are you going? Make a numbered list of the places you intend to go. Now you can practice two important sets of vocabulary at the same time. You can also think about grouping this vocabulary into logical sets. Which places involve travel? Which places involve recreation? ¡Vámonos!

English	Español	Guide
Airport	Aeropuerto	ah-eh-row-poo-**AIR**-toe
Bakery	Panadería	pan-ah-day-**REE**-ah
Bank	Banco	**BAN**-co
Barber shop	Peluquería	pay-loo-kay-**REE**-ah
Beauty salon	Salón de belleza	sa-**LAWN** day bay-**YEA**-sa
Church	Iglesia	e-**GLAY**-see-ah
City hall	Municipio	moon-knee-**SEE**-p-oh
Fire department	Departamento de bomberos	day-par-ta-**MEN**-toe day bom-**BAY**-rows
Florist	Florería	floor-ray-**REE**-ah
Gas station	Gasolinera	gas-so-lee-**NAY**-rah
Grocery store	Grosería	gros-eh-**REE**-ah

English	Español	Guide
Hospital	Hospital	os-p-**TAL**
Hotel	Hotel	oh-**TEL**
Jewelry store	Joyería	hoy-eh-**REE**-ah
Laundromat	Lavandería	la-van-day-**REE**-an
Library	Biblioteca	b-lee-oh-**TECK**-ah
Market	Mercado	mare-**CA**-doe
Movie theatre	Cine	**SEEN**-nay
Museum	Museo	moo-**SAY**-oh
Park	Parque	**PAR**-kay
Pharmacy	Farmacia	far-**MA**-see-ah
Police station	Estación de policía	es-ta-see-**ON** day po-lee-**SEE**-ah
Post office	Correo	core-**A**-oh
Restaurant	Restaurante	res-tower-**AHN**-tay
School	Escuela	es-coo-**A**-la
Shoe store	Zapatería	sa-pa-tay-**REE**-ah
Store	Tienda	t-**N**-da
Super market	Super mercado	soo-**PEAR** mare-**CA**-doe
Theatre	Teatro	tay-**AH**-trow
Train station	Estación de tren	es-ta-see-**ON** day tren

Traveling from Place to Place

Traveling to locations in Latin America for mission work or vacations is becoming very popular. It's easy to see why. Trips to Mexico, Central and South America can be reasonably priced and almost everywhere in Latin American that you look, help is needed. No matter where you travel or what your purpose is, there will be much to do and see, not to mention all the people you will talk to! To hit the road running when you arrive, the following is a list of handy vocabulary that you will need the minute you step off your flight.

English	Español	Guide
Airline	Aerolínea	ah-eh-row-LEAN-nay-ah
Airplane	Avión	ah-v-ON
Airport	Aeropuerto	ah-eh-row-poo-AIR-toe
Aisle	Pasillo	pa-SEE-yo
Arrival	Llegada	yea-GA-da
Barrage claim	Reclamo de equipaje	ray-CLAM-oh day eh-key-PA-hey
Bathroom	Baño Servicio	BAHN-yo ser-V-see-oh
Bus	Autobús	ow-toe-BOOS

English	Español	Guide
Bus station	Estación de autobuses	es-sta-see-ON day ow-toe-BOOS-ace
Car	Carro	CA-row
Carry-on-baggage	Equipaje de mano	eh-key-PA-hey day MA-no
Customs	Aduana	ah-do-AHN-na
Departure/Exit/Gate	Salida	sa-LEE-da
Destination	Destinación	des-t-na-see-ON
Flight	Vuelto	voo-EL-toe
Lost and found	Oficina de objetos perdidos	oh-fee-SEEN-na day ob-HEY-toes pear-D-dose
Money exchange	Cambio	CAM-b-oh
Reservation	Reserva	ray-SER-va
Row	Fila	FEE-la
Seat	Asiento	ah-see-N-toe
Security	Seguridad	say-goo-ree-DAD
Taxi	Taxi	TAX-e
Terminal	Terminal	ter-me-NAL
Ticket	Boleto	bow-LAY-toe
Transportation	Transportación	trans-por-ta-see-ON
Train station	Estación de tren	es-sta-see-ON day tren
Subway	Metro	MAY-tro

Buying Clothes

¡Venta! Everyone loves a sale. If you're traveling in Latin America, you could find yourself at a large flea market that's filled with exotic items or a department store with bargains of all sorts that you would not be able to find easily in the United States. This vocabulary will help you purchase clothing and find the best deals and discounts.

English	Español	Guide
Bathing suit	Traje de baño	TRAH-hey day BAHN-yo
Belt	Cinturón	seen-too-RHONE
Boots	Botas	BOW-tas
Dress	Vestido	ves-T-doe
Gloves	Guantes	goo-AHN-tays
Hat	Sombrero	som-BRAY-row
Jacket	Chaqueta	cha-KAY-ta
Jeans	Jeans Vaqueros	Jeans va-KAY-rows
Overcoat	Abrigo	ah-BREE-go
Pants	Pantalones	pan-ta-LONE-ace
Pajamas	Pijamas	p-HA-mas
Raincoat	Impermeable	eem-pear-may-AH-blay
Robe	Bata	BA-ta
Sandals	Sandalias	san-DAL-e-ahs
Scarf	Bufanda	boo-FAHN-da

English	Español	Guide
Shirt	Camisa	ca-**ME**-sa
Shoes	Zapatos	sa-**PA**-toes
Shorts	Pantalones cortos	pan-ta-**LONE**-ace **CORE**-toes
Skirt	Falda	**FALL**-da
Sneakers	Tenis	**TAY**-knees
Socks	Calcetines	cal-say-**TEEN**-ace
Suit	Traje	**TRAH**-hey
Sweater	Suéter	sue-**A**-ter
Tie	Corbata	core-**BA**-ta
T-shirt	Camiseta	ca-me-**SET**-ta
Umbrella	Paraguas	**PA**-ra-**AH**-goo-wahs
Underwear	Ropa interior	**ROW**-pa een-tay-ree-**OR**
Vest	Chaleco	cha-**LAY**-co

Tips & Tidbits

Dress very conservatively on your mission trip. Do not take "short" shorts, mini-skirts, revealing shirts, or clothing that is too tight. Latin Americans dress much more conservatively than most of us do. Going out to dinner or to a party calls for much dressier attire than it does in the US. Rather than running the risk of offending your Latin American hosts, it's best to leave contemporary "style" at home. Also leave expensive jewelry at home. It's impolite to make ostentacious shows of wealth.

Parts of the Body

Many mission trips provide vital medical and dental care. Your knowledge of these basic parts of human anatomy will give you and the person you are treating more confidence. Speaking even *un poquito español* in this situation will also help you build a more trusting relationship with your patient and their family members. Use basic layman's terms as much as possible.

English	Español	Guide
Abdomen	Abdomen	ab-**DOE**-men
Ankle	Tobillo	toe-**B**-yo
Arm	Brazo	**BRA**-so
Back	Espalda	es-**PALL**-doe
Body	Cuerpo	coo-**AIR**-poe
Brain	Cerebro	say-**RAY**-bro
Chest	Pecho	**PAY**-cho
Chin	Barbilla	bar-**B**-ya
Ear	Oreja	oh-**RAY**-ha
Eye	Ojo	**OH**-ho
Face	Cara	**CA**-ra
Finger	Dedo	**DAY**-do
Foot	Pie	**P**-ay
Hand	Mano	**MA**-no
Head	Cabeza	ca-**BAY**-sa
Heart	Corazón	core-ra-**SEWN**
Knee	Rodilla	row-**D**-ya

English	Español	Guide
Leg	Pierna	p-**YAIR**-na
Mouth	Boca	**BOW**-ca
Nail	Uña	**OON**-ya
Neck	Cuello	coo-**A**-yo
Nose	Nariz	na-**REECE**
Skin	Piel	p-**L**
Shoulder	Hombro	**ON**-bro
Spine	Espina	es-**P**-na
Throat	Garganta	gar-**GAN**-ta
Toe	Dedo del pie	**DAY**-doe del **P**-a
Tooth	Diente	d-**N**-tay
Wrist	Muñeca	moon-**YEA**-ca

The Internal Organs — Los Órganos Internos

English	Español	Guide
Anus	Ano	**AH**-no
Appendix	Apéndice	ah-**PEN**-d-say
Colon	Colón	co-**LOAN**
Diaphragm	Diafragma	d-ah-**FRAG**-mo
Esophagus	Esófago	es-**SO**-fa-go
Gall bladder	Vesícula billar	vay-**C**-coo-la b-lee-**ARE**
Heart	Corazón	co-rah-**SEWN**
Kidney	Riñón	reen-**YON**
Large intestine	Intestino grueso	een-tes-**T**-no grew-**A**-so

75

English	Español	Guide
Liver	Hígado	E-ga-doe
Lung	Pulmón	pool-MOAN
Rectum	Recto	WRECK-toe
Small intestine	Intestino delgado	een-tes-T-no del-GA-doe
Stomach	Estómago	es-TOE-ma-go

The Mouth — La Boca

English	Español	Guide
Canine	Diente canino	d-N-tay ca-KEEN-no
Gum	Encía	n-SEE-ah
Hard palate	Paladar duro	pa-la-DAR DO-row
Incisor	Diente incisivo	d-N-tay
Molar	Muela	moo-WAY-la
	Molar	no-LAR
Soft palate	Paladar blando	pa-la-DAR
Teeth	Dientes	d-N-tays
Tongue	Lengua	LENG-goo-ah

Tips & Tidbits

In some Latin American countries medical clinics are scarce. Patients and their families will walk for hours to get to the closest one. Once they arrive, there is often no medicine for them or doctor to treat them.

Providing Dental Exams

Because of the nature of your work with children on this trip, the verbs in this section are conjugated informally. When working with adults, simply drop the "s" from the ending of the verb. Example: tienes *(informal)* tiene *(formal)*.

English	Español	Guide
Do you have a tooth ache?	¿Tienes dolor de dientes?	t-N-nace doe-LORE day d-N-tays
You have a decayed tooth.	Tienes un diente cariado.	t-N-nace oon d-N-tay ca-ree-AH-doe
You have an abscess.	Tienes un absceso.	t-N-nace oon ab-SAY-so
Do your teeth hurt?	¿Los dientes le duelen?	los d-N-tays lay do-WAY-len
Which tooth hurts?	Indique el diente donde tienes dolor.	n-D-kay l d-N-tay DON-day t-N-ace doe-LORE
Is the pain a problem during the night?	Durante la noche, ¿es el dolor un problema?	do-RAHN-tay la NO-chay es l doe-LORE oon pro-BLAY-ma
I need to remove the tooth.	Necesito sacar el diente.	nay-say-SEE-toe sa-CAR l d-N-tay

English	Español	Guide
I need to remove (1, 2, 3) teeth.	Necesito sacar (uno, dos, tres) diente *(s)*.	nay-say-SEE-toe sa-CAR (OO-no, dose, trays) d-N-tays
You need an injection to numb your tooth.	Necesitas una inyección adormecer el diente.	nay-say-SEE-tahs OO-na n-yeck-see-ON ah-door-may-SER l d-N-tay
Have you ever had a tooth pulled before?	¿Ha tenido un diente sacó antes?	ah ten-KNEE-doe oon d-N-tay sa-CO AHN-tays
You are going to feel a small sting.	Vas a sentir una quemazón pequeña.	vas ah sen-TEAR OO-na kay-ma-SEWN pay-CANE-ya
You are going to have a little pain.	Vas a tener un poco de dolor.	vas ah sen-TEAR oon PO-co day doe-LORE
I'm going to make the injection more comfortable with this ointment.	Voy a hacer la inyección más cómoda para ti con este ungüento	voy a ah-SER la n-yeck-see-ON mas CO-mo-da PA-rah tee con ES-tay oon-GWEN-toe
Here comes the sting.	Aquí viene la quemazón.	ah-KEY v-N-a la kay-ma-SEWN
You need another injection.	Necesitas otra inyección.	nay-say-SEE-tas OH-trah n-yeck-see-ON

78

English	Español	Guide
Your tooth is loose.	Tu diente está flojo.	to d-N-tay es-TA FLOW-ho
I will wiggle your tooth before removing it.	Voy a mover tu diente antes que sacándolo.	voy ah mo-VAIR to d-N-tay AHN-tays kay sa-CAN-doe-low
I have to loosen your tooth before I remove it.	Tengo que aflojar tu diente antes que sacándolo.	TANG-go kay ah-flow-HAR to d-N-tay AHN-tays kay sa-CAN-doe-low
You will feel pressure.	Vas a sentir una presión pequeña.	vas ah sen-TEAR OO-na pray-see-ON pay-CANE-ya
You are doing well.	Estás muy bien.	es-TAHS mooy b-N
Bite on this.	Favor de morder esta.	fa-VOR day more-DARE ES-ta
Avoid cold or hot drinks	Evites bebidas frías o calientes.	a-V-tace bay-B-das FREE-ahs oh ca-lee-N-tace
Avoid chewing hard foods.	Evites masticar comidas duras.	a-V-tace ma-stee-CAR co-ME-das DO-rahs

Are You in Pain? — ¿Tiene Dolor?

When a Spanish-speaking patient discusses pain and discomfort, it's expressed differently than it is in English. Rather than *being* in pain, *en español* you *have* pain. Refer to the chapter on irregular verbs for more uses of *tener*. Frequently, you will hear the words *tengo dolor*, which means *I have* pain. This phrase is followed by the word for the affected area. When you are asking if the patient is in pain, use the phrase ¿*tiene dolor?*

English	Español	Guide
Does it hurt?	¿Le duele?	lay do-**A**-lay
Where?	¿Dónde?	**DON**-day
Show me.	Indícalo.	een-**D**-ca-low
It hurts.	Me duele.	may do-**A**-lay
They hurt.	Me duelen	may do-**A**-lynn
Do you have pain?	¿Tiene dolor?	t-**N**-a doe-**LORE**
Do you have a lot of pain?	¿Tiene mucho dolor?	t-**N**-a **MOO**-cho doe-**LORE**
Is the pain mild?	¿Tiene dolor moderado?	t-**N**-a doe-**LORE** mo-dare-**RAH**-doe
Is the pain intermittent?	¿Tiene dolor intermitente?	t-**N**-a doe-**LORE** n-ter-me-**TENT**-tay
Is the pain deep?	¿Tiene dolor profundo?	t-**N**-a doe-**LORE** pro-**FOON**-doe
Is the pain constant?	¿Tiene dolor constante?	t-**N**-a doe-**LORE** con-**STAN**-tay

English	Español	Guide
Is the pain burning?	¿Tiene dolor quemante?	t-N-a doe-**LORE** kay-**MAN**-tay
Is the pain severe?	¿Tiene dolor muy fuerte?	t-N-a doe-**LORE** foo-**AIR**-tay
Is the pain throbbing?	¿Tiene dolor pulsante?	t-N-a doe-**LORE** pull-**SAN**-tay

Diseases — Enfermedades

In this list of common diseases, the strong relationship between our two languages is *obvio*, isn't it? Here's a tip to help you get started. Diseases which end in the suffix "*-itis*," like arthritis, bursitis, and tendonitis will be essentially the same words in Spanish. If the words aren't identical, try using the Latin roots from your medical studies.

English	Español	Guide
Anemia	Anemia	ah-**NAY**-me-ah
Appendicitis	Apendicitis	ah-pen-d-**SEE**-tees
Arthritis	Artritis	are-**TREE**-tees
Asthma	Asma	**AS**-ma
Bronchitis	Bronquitis	bron-**KEY**-tees
Cancer	Cáncer	**KAHN**-cer
Chicken pox	Varicela	va-ree-**SAY**-la
Cold	Catarro	ca-**TAR**-row

English	Español	Guide
Diabetes	Diabetes	d-ah-**BAY**-tes
Fever	Fiebre	fee-**A**-bray
Flu	Influenza	n-flew-**N**-sa
Gall stones	Cálculos en la vesícula	**CAL**-coo-lows n la vay-**SEE**-coo-la
Glaucoma	Glaucoma	gl-ow-**CO**-ma
Hay fever	Fiebre de heno	fee-**A**-bray day **A**-no
Hepatitis	Hepatitis	ape-ah-**T**-tis
Herpes	Herpes	**AIR**-pays
Hives	Urticaria	oor-t-**CA**-ree-ah
Hypoglycemia	Hipoglucemia	ee-po-glue-**SAY**-me-ah
Indigestion	Indigestión	n-dee-hess-t-**ON**
Jaundice	Ictericia	ick-tay-**REE**-see-ah
Kidney stones	Cálculos en los riñones	**CAL**-coo-lows n los reen-**NYO**-nays
Laryngitis	Laringitis	la-reen-**HE**-tees
Leukemia	Leucemia	lay-oo-**SAY**-me-ah
Measles	Sarampión	sa-ram-pee-**ON**
Mumps	Paperas	pa-**PEAR**-rahs
Pneumonia	Pulmonía	pool-mo-**KNEE**-ah
Tuberculosis	Tuberculosis	too-bear-coo-**LOW**-sis

Other Common Problems

If your patient has something which is going to require further treatment, here is a list of common symptoms and conditions that you may encounter. Knowing this list of terms will help you make a correct diagnosis *rápido!*

English	Español	Guide
Abscess	Absceso	ab-SAY-so
Blister	Ampolla	am-PO-ya
Broken bone	Hueso roto	who-AY-so ROW-toe
	Fractura	frac-TOO-rah
Bruise	Contusión	con-too-see-ON
Bump	Hinchazón	eem-cha-SEWN
Burn	Quemadura	kay-ma-DO-ra
Chills	Escalofrío	es-ca-low-FREE-oh
Cough	Tos	toes
Cramps	Calambre	ca-LAMB-bray
Diarrhea	Diarrea	dee-ah-RAY-ah
Fever	Fiebre	fee-A-bray
Lump	Bulto	BOOL-toe
Migraine	Migraña	me-GRAN-ya
Rash	Erupción	a-roop-see-ON
Sprain	Torcedura	tor-say-DO-ra
Swelling	Inflamación	een-fla-ma-see-ON
Wound	Herido	a-REE-doe

Remedies and Medicines
Remedios y Medicinas

You are going to be pleasantly surprised when you see all the English Spanish matches or *cognates* in this list of remedies and medicines. These are your *amigos!*

English	Español	Guide
Tablet	Tableta	ta-**BLAY**-ta
Capsule	Cápsula	**CAP**-soo-la
Pill	Píldora	**PEEL**-dor-ah
Lozenge	Pastilla	pahs-**T**-ya
Analgesic	Analgésico	ah-nal-**HEY**-see-co
Anesthetic	Anestésico	ah-nay-**STAY**-see-co
Antacid	Antiácido	ahn-t-**AH**-see-doe
Antibiotic	Antibiótico	ahn-t-b-**OH**-t-co
Anticoagulant	Anticoagulante	ahn-t-co-ah-goo-**LAN**-tay
Antidote	Antídoto	ahn-**T**-oh-doe
Antihistamine	Antihistamínicos	ahn-t-ees-ta-**MEAN**-knee-cos
Anti-inflammatory	Anti-inflamatorio	ahn-t-een-fla-ma-**TOR**-ree-oh
Antiseptic	Antiséptico	ahn-t-**SEP**-t-co
Aspirin	Aspirina	ahs-p-**REE**-na
Astringent	Astringente	ah-streen-**HEN**-tay

84

English	Español	Guide
Barbiturate	Barbitúrico	bar-b-**TOO**-ree-co
Chemotherapy	Quimioterapia	key-me-oh-ter-**RA**-p-ah
Codeine	Codeína	co-day-**EE**-na
Contraceptive	Contraceptivo	con-tra-cep-T-vo
Cough drop	Pastillas para la tos	pas-T-yas **PA**-ra la toes
Cough syrup	Jarabe para la tos	ha-**RA**-bay **PA**-ra la toes
Cortisone	Cortisona	core-tee-**SO**-na
Cream	Crema	**CRAY**-ma
Diuretic	Diurético	d-oo-**RAY**-t-co
Disinfectant	Desinfectante	des-een-fec-**TAN**-tay
Inhaler	Inhalador	n-ah-la-**DOOR**
Insulin	Insulina	n-soo-**LEAN**-ah
Laxative	Laxante	lax-**AN**-tay
Liniment	Linimento	lean-knee-**MEN**-toe
Lotion	Loción	lo-see-**ON**
Morphine	Morfina	more-**FEE**-na
Narcotic	Narcótico	nar-**CO**-t-co
Nitroglycerine	Nitroglicerina	knee-tro-glee-ser-**REE**-na
Penicillin	Penicilina	pay-knee-see-**LEE**-na
Sedative	Sedante	say-**DAN**-tay
Solution	Solución	so-lou-see-**ON**

85

English	Español	Guide
Steroid	Esteroide	es-stair-ROY-day
Suppository	Supositorio	sue-po-see-TOR-ree-oh
Tranquilizer	Tranquilizante	tran-key-lee-SAN-tay
Vaccine	Vacuna	va-COO-na
Vitamin	Vitamina	v-ta-ME-na

Side Effects — Efectos Adversos

After prescribing a medication for your patient, your next step will be discussing possible side effects. In *español* there are several ways to address the term "side effects." You can be quite literal and call them bad or adverse effects, like the title of this section demonstrates. In addition, the phrase "bad reaction" or *mala reacción* is also used.

English	Español	Guide
Allergie	Alergia	al-LAIR-he-ah
Anxiety	Ansiedad	an-see-a-DAD
Bad reaction	Mala reacción	MAL-ah ray-ax-see-ON
Bleeding	Sangrado	san-GRA-doe
Constipation	Estreñimiento	es-train-knee-me-N-toe
Decreased appetite	Disminución del apetito	dis-me-new-see-ON del ah-pay-T-toe

English	Español	Guide
Dizziness	Mareos	ma-**RAY**-ohs
	Vértigo	**VER**-t-go
Dry mouth	Boca seca	**BOW**-ca **SAY**-ca
Headache	Dolor de cabeza	doe-**LORE** day ca-**BAY**-sa
High blood pressure	Presión sanguínea alta	pray-see-**ON** san-**GWEE**-nay-ah **AL**-ta
Hives	Ronchas de la piel	**RON**-chas day la p-**L**
Increased appetite	Aumento del apetito	ow-**MEN**-toe del ah-pay-**T**-toe
Insomnia	Insomnio	n-**SOM**-knee-oh
Itching	Picazón	p-ca-**SEWN**
Low blood pressure	Presión sanguínea baja	pray-see-**ON** san-**GWEE**-nay-ah **BAA**-ha
Sleepiness	Sueño	sue-**AY**-nyo

Dispensing Instructions — Las Instrucciones

Here's an important tip on your choice of phrases to use when you are double-checking to make sure that your Spanish-speaking patient has understood the instructions you have given them pertaining to a medication. Always use the phrase "do you understand my instructions." This is much better than asking "do you understand my directions." Remember that a *dirección* in *español* is an *address*.

English	Español	Guide
Prescription	Receta médica	ray-SAY-ta MAY-d-ka
	Fórmula	FOR-moo-la
	Receta	ray-SAY-ta
Take the medicine	Toma la medicina	TOE-ma la may-d-SEEN-na
Before meals	Antes de las comidas	AN-tays day las co-ME-das
Between meals	Entre las comidas	N-tray las co-ME-das
After meals	Después de las comidas	days-poo-ACE day las co-ME-das
In the morning	Por la mañana	pour la man-YA-na
In the afternoon	Por la tarde	pour la TAR-day
In the evening	Por la noche	pour la NO-chay
At bedtime	A la hora de acostarse	ah la OR-ah day ah-co-STAR-say
Only when you have pain	Solo cuando tiene dolor	SO-low coo-AN-doe t-N-a doe-LORE
As directed by your doctor	Según las instrucciones de su doctor.	say-GOON las n-strook-see-ON-ace day sue doc-TOR
With water	Con agua	con AH-goo-ah
With milk	Con leche	con LAY-chay
With food	Con la comida	con la co-ME-da

English	Español	Guide
With breakfast	Con el desayuno	con L day-say-OO-no
With lunch	Con el almuerzo	con L al-moo-AIR-so
With dinner	Con la cena	con la SAY-na
On an empty stomach	Con el estómago vacío.	con l es-TOE-ma-go va-SEE-oh
Only when necessary	Solo cuando es necesario	SO-low coo-AN-doe ace nay-say-SAR-ree-oh
Take the medicine # times per day.	Toma la medicina # veces por día.	TOE-ma la may-d-SEEN-na # VASE-aces pour D-ah

How Much and How Often — Cuánto y Cuándo

Dispensing instructions can be extremely confusing to patients, and when you are prescribing in Latin America, it could be confusing to you too, because you must give the amounts using the metric system. This vocabulary and the conversion chart is on the following page will help you.

English	Español	Guide
Take	Toma	TOE-ma
One teaspoon	Una cucharadita	OO-na coo-char-ra-D-ta

89

English	Español	Guide
½ teaspoon	Una media cucharadita	OO-na may-D-ah coo-char-ra-D-ta
One tablespoon	Una cucharada	OO-na coo-char-RA-da
A cup	Una copa	OO-na CO-pa
Half	Una media	OO-na may-D-ah
A drop	Una gota	OO-na GO-ta
Apply	Aplique	ah-PLEA-kay
Sparingly	Poquito	po-KEY-toe
Affected areas	Áreas afectados	AH-ray-as ah-fec-TA-das
Shake well.	Agítese bien.	ah-HE-tay-say b-N
External use	Uso externo	OO-so x-TER-no
Keep refrigerated.	Guarda en el refrigerador.	goo-WAHR-da in l ray-free-hair-ray-DOOR
Liter	Litro	LEE-tro
Milliliter	Mililitro	me-lee-LEE-tro
Gram	Gramo	GRA-mo
Kilo	Kilo	KEY-low

Tips & Tidbits: Converting Doses into Metrics

¼ tsp. = 1 ml.　　　　　　½ tsp. = 2 ml.

1 tsp. = 5 ml.　　　　　　1 tbsp. = 15 ml

¼ C. = 50 ml.　　　　　　1/3 C. = 75 ml.

½ C = 125 ml.　　　　　　2/3 C. = 150 ml.

¾ C = 175 ml.　　　　　　1 C. = 250 ml.

1 pt. = 500 ml.　　　　　　1 qt. = 1 liter

When   Cuándo

English	Español	Guide
Take ____ times	Toma ____ veces	TOE-ma ____ VAY-says
Every day	Cada día	CA-da DEE-ah
Until finished	Hasta que se termina	AH-sta kay say ter-ME-na
Every ___ hours	Cada ____ horas	CA-da ____ OR-ahs
____times per day	____ veces al día	____VAY-says al DEE-ah
For ____ days	Por ____ días	pour ____ DEE-ahs
For ____ weeks	Por ____ semanas	pour ____say-MAN-nas
For ____ months	Por ____ meses	pour ____MAY-says

Giving Instructions — Las Instrucciones

Using the "command" form of verbs can often be a delicate undertaking. Most of us don't see ourselves as drill sergeants, but we still need to give people instructions in a firmly and yet gently. To make command forms in Spanish, you are essentially taking AR verbs and using ER endings with them. In other words, if the verb would normally end with the letter "a" in the *usted* form, to make a command, you should end the verb with an "e" instead. For regular ER verbs do the opposite and end the verb with the letter "a".

91

Many verbs that are used in dealing with patients are known as reflexive verbs. This means that the action falls back upon the subject. We used to do this all the time in English. I'm sure you've heard phrases like: I'm going to sit myself down or I'm going to bathe myself. The use of *myself* indicates that the verb is reflexive. When you see the following examples, look for the little "se" on the end of the Spanish verb. That's a clear sign that this verb is reflexive. That means it's in a class by itself.

English	Español	Guide
Sit down	Siéntese	see-**N**-tay-say
Stand up	Levántese	lay-**VAN**-tay-say
Breathe deeply.	Respire profundo.	ray-**SPEE**-ray pro-**FOON**-doe
Take a deep breath.	Aspire profundo.	ahs-**PIER**-ray pro-**FOON**-doe
Open your mouth.	Abre la boca.	**AH**-bray la **BOW**-ca
Get undressed.	Desvístase	days-**VEES**-ta-say
Lie down.	Acuéstese.	ah-coo-**ACE**-tay-say
Turn around.	Voltéese	vol-**TAY**-a-say
Wait	Espérese	es-**PAY**-ray-say
Come here	Venga aquí.	**VEN**-ga ah-**KEY**
Get up	Súbase	**SOO**-ba-say
Get up on the table.	Súbase a la mesa.	**SOO**-ba-say ah la **MAY**-sa
Calm down.	Cálmese	**CAL**-may-say

Eating in Latin America

Cuisine in Latin America is as diverse as the people are. Meals are based on typical products found in each country or region. When many Americans think about Latin American foods, some think of only Mexican food, but there is a much wider diversity of tastes and dishes than that!

Meals and Beverages

English	Español	Guide
Meal or food	Comida	co-ME-da
Breakfast	Desayuno	day-say-OO-no
Lunch	Almuerzo	al-moo-AIR-so
Dinner	Cena	SAY-na
Dessert	Postre	POS-tray
Snack	Merienda	may-ree-N-da
Beer	Cerveza	ser-VAY-sa
Beverage	Bebida	bay-B-da
Coffee	Café	ca-FAY
Juice	Jugo	WHO-go
Red wine	Vino tinto	V-no TEEN-toe
Salad	Ensalada	n-sa-LA-da
Soft drink	Refresco	ray-FRES-co
Soup	Sopa	SO-pa
Tea	Té	tay
Water	Agua	AH-goo-ah
White wine	Vino blanco	VEE-no BLAN-co

Meats and Seafood — Carne y Mariscos

In most Latin American countries meat is very expensive. For most families beef is not often affordable. Poultry, pork and seafood are more common in day-to-day meals, but most of the time some sort of dried bean serves as the family's source of daily protein. Make sure to try everything your hosts prepare for you while on your mission trip. In many cases having the extra mouths to feed of your team is stretching the community's resources to the limit.

English	Español	Guide
Meat	Carne	**CAR**-nay
Beef	Carne de vaca	**CAR**-nay day **VA**-ca
Chicken	Pollo	**POE**-yo
Fish	Pescado	pace-**KA**-doe
Ham	Jamón	ha-**MON**
Hamburger	Hamburguesa	am-burr-**GAY**-sa
Hot Dog	Perro caliente	**PAY**-row ca-lee-**N**-tay
Pork chop	Chuleta de puerco	chew-**LAY**-ta day poo-**AIR**-co
Sausage	Salchicha	sal-**CHI**-cha
Seafood	Mariscos	ma-**REES**-cos
Steak	Bistec	**BEE**-stek
Tuna	Atún	ah-**TOON**
Turkey	Pavo	**PA**-vo

Fruits — Frutas

When you begin to taste the amazing array of fruits that are readily available in Latin America, you may think that you have landed in the Garden of Eden! Fruit is plentiful, fresh and delicious. You will be pleasantly surprised at the variety you find. Did you know that there are twenty-three different varieties of banana which grow in Latin America?

English	Español	Guide
Fruit	Fruta	FRU-ta
Apple	Manzana	man-SAN-na
Banana	Plátano	PLA-ta-no
Cantaloupe	Melón	may-LOAN
	Cantalupo	can-ta-LOO-poe
Coconut	Coco	CO-co
Grape	Uva	OO-va
Grapefruit	Toronja	toe-ROON-ha
Lemon	Limón	lee-MON
Lime	Lima	LEE-ma
Mango	Mango	MAN-go
Orange	Naranja	na-RAN-ha
Papaya	Papaya	pa-PIE-ya
Peach	Melocotón	may-low-co-TON
Pear	Pera	PAY-rah
Pineapple	Piña	PEEN-ya
Raisin	Pasita	pa-SEE-ta
Strawberry	Fresa	FRAY-sa

English	Español	Guide
Tamarind	Tamarindo	ta-ma-**REEN**-doe
Watermelon	Sandía	san-**DEE**-ah

Vegetables — Vegetales

Many Latin American diets are rich in fresh fruits and vegetables, some of which are cooked in very interesting ways. For example, in Mexico a delicious candy called *camote* is prepared from sweet potatoes. Its rich orange color makes it perfect for autumn treats. Sauces are made from an array of chilis and herbs. Dried pumpkin seeds are crushed and used in sauces called *moles*. This sauce is extremely complex—and delicious. It usually consists of more than twenty ingredients including chocolate!

English	Español	Guide
Vegetable	Vegetal	vay-he-**TAL**
Avocado	Aguacate	agua-**CA**-tay
Dried Beans	Frijoles	free-**HO**-lace
Black beans	Frijoles negros	free-**HO**-lace **NAY**-grows
Broccoli	Brócoli	**BRO**-co-lee
Carrot	Zanahoria	sa-na-**OR**-ree-ah
Cauliflower	Coliflor	co-lee-**FLOOR**
Celery	Apio	**AH**-p-oh
Corn	Maíz	ma-**EES**
Cucumber	Pepino	pay-**P**-no

English	Español	Guide
Green bean	Ejote	a-HOE-tay
Green bell pepper	Pimiento verde	p-me-N-toe VER-day
Green peas	Guisantes	gee-SAN-tays
Lettuce	Lechuga	lay-CHEW-ga
Mushroom	Champiñón	cham-peen-YON
Onion	Cebolla	say-BOY-ya
Potato	Patata	pa-TA-ta
Pumpkin	Calabaza	ca-la-BA-sa
Squash	Calabacera	ca-la-ba-SER-rah
Sweet potato	Camote	ca-MO-tay
Tomato	Tomate	to-MA-tay

Dairy and Egg Products

English	Español	Guide
Butter	Mantequilla	man-tay-KEY-ya
Cheese	Queso	KAY-so
Cream	Crema	CRAY-ma
Egg	Huevo	oo-WAVE-oh
Half and half	Leche con crema	LAY-che con CRAY-ma
Hard-boiled egg	Huevo duro	oo-WAVE-oh DO-row
Ice-cream	Helado	a-LA-doe
Milk	Leche	LAY-che

English	Español	Guide
Sour cream	Crema de leche agria	CRAY-ma day LAY-che ah-GREE-ah
Yogurt	Yogurt	yo-GOOR

Bread, Pasta and Desserts

Latin American breads and desserts tend to be a bit less sweet than most of the decadent ones we enjoy in the US. Perhaps it's the tropical climate that makes eating lighter foods more appealing or the array of lucious fruits, nevertheless, the sweets you try will definately be a treat!

English	Español	Guide
Bread	Pan	pahn
Cake	Pastel	pas-TELL
	Queque	KAY-kay
Candy	Dulce	DOOL-say
Cereal	Cereal	say-ray-AL
Chips	Tostaditas	tos-ta-D-tas
Chocolate	Chocolate	cho-co-LA-tay
Cookie	Galleta	ga-YEA-ta
Cracker	Galleta salada	ga-YEA-ta sa-LA-da
Custard	Flan	flahn
Honey	Miel	mee-L
Ice cream	Helado	a-LA-doe

English	Español	Guide
Jam	Mermelada	mer-may-**LA**-da
Peanut butter	Crema de cacahuate	**CRAY**-ma day ca-ca-who-**A**-tay
Pie	Tarta	**TAR**-ta
Pudding	Pudín	poo-**DEAN**
Rice	Arroz	ah-**ROHS**

Instructions - Instrucciones

Whether you are working on a construction site during a mission trip or in the US, being able to give instructions, ask for help or for tools will be important to your success and efficiency. The following is a list of common instructions. Always add *por favor* or please to your *instrucciones*! Spanish is a language of courtesy and that's extremely important to remember on your mission trip or anywhere else.

English	Español	Guide
Come here	Venga aquí	**VEN**-ga ah-**KEY**.
Let's go	Vámonos	**VA**-mo-nos
Wait	Espere	es-**PEAR**-ray
Stop	Pare	**PAR**-ray
Help me	Ayúdeme	ay-**U**-day-may
Help him	Ayúdelo	ay-**U**-day-low
Like this	Así	ah-**SEE**

English	Español	Guide
Not like this	Así no	ah-SEE no
Show me	Muéstreme	moo-ES-tray-may
Good	Bien	b-N
Point to it	Indíquelo	n-DEE-kay-low
Move that here	Mueve eso aquí	moo-wavy ES-so ah-KEY
Bring me that	Tráigame eso	try-GA-may ES-toe
Give it to me	Démelo	DAY-may-low
To the right	A la derecha	a la day-RAY-cha
To the left.	A la izquierda	a la ees-kay-AIR-da
Remove these.	Quite estos	KEY-tay ES-toes
Pick up all these.	Recoja todo estos	ray-CO-ha TOE-dos ES-toes
Put it there.	Póngalo allí	PON-ga-low ah-YE
Inside	Dentro	DEN-tro
Under	Debajo	day-BA-ho
Carry this.	Lleve esto.	YEA-vay ES-toe
Open	Abra,	AH-bra.
Close	Cierre	c-EH-ray
Now	Ahora	ah-ORA
Later.	Más tarde.	mas TAR-day
Here	Aquí	ah-KEY
There	Allí	ah-YE

100

Los Pies y Las Pulgadas
Feet and Inches

Un pie	A foot
Una pulgada	An inch
Una yarda	A yard

A tape measure = La cinta métrica or un metro
A measurement = Una medida

1/16"	Un decimosexto de pulgada
1/8"	Un octavo de pulgada
1/4"	Un cuarto de pulgada
1/2"	Una media de pulgada
3/4	Tres cuartos de pulgada

T-square   La escuadra

A board 6 feet long and 4 inches wide
Una tabla seis pies de larga y cuatro pulgadas de ancha.

6 feet long4 inches wide
Seis pies de larga cuatro pulgadas de ancha

Smaller	más pequeño	Darker	más oscuro
Longer	más largo	More	más
Shorter	más corto	Less	menos
Lighter	más claro		

Tips & Tidbits
Latin America uses the metric system for measurements.

The Tools of the Trade

When you attempt to learn a long list of vocabulary, it's easy to get overwhelmed in the process. I always tell my *amigos*  that learning a long list of new words is just like learning to eat a steak. That's right! It's hard to eat the whole thing at once, so we cut it into bite-sized pieces. Spanish is learned much the same way. You have to organize the material and prioritize it. Chew on it a little at a time; then move on to the next bite when you are ready. Go at your own pace, and try not to rush the learning process.

English	Español	Guide
Ax	Hacha	AH-cha
Barrel	Barril	bar-REEL
Board	Tabla de Madera	ta-BLA day ma-DARE-ah
Bolts	Pernos	PEAR-nose
Box	Caja	CA-ha
Broom	Escoba	es-CO-bah
Brush (paint)	Brocha	BRO-cha
Bucket	Cubo	COO-bow
Cable	Cable	CA-blay
Can	Lata	LA-ta
Canvas or tarp	Lona	LOW-na
Caulk	Sellador	say-YA-door
Cement block	Bloque de cemento	BLOW-kay day say-MEN-toe

English	Español	Guide
Chicken wire	Alambrada	ah-lam-**BRA**-da
Chisel	Cincel	seen-**CELL**
Clamp	Pinza	**PEEN**-sa
Compressor	Compresor	com-pres-**OR**
Concrete	Concreto	con-**CRAY**-toe
Crowbar	Barra	**BAR**-ah
Cutter	Cortador	core-ta-**DOOR**
Drill	Barrena, taladro	bar-**A**-na ta-**LA**-drow
Drill bit	Broca	**BRO**-ka
File	Lima	**LEE**-ma
Extension cord	Cable de extensión	**CA**-bley day x-ten-see-**ON**
Glue	Goma	**GO**-ma
Gravel	Grava	**GRA**-ba
Hammer	Martillo	mar-**T**-yo
Hack saw	Sierra para cortar metal	see-**AIR**-ah **PA**-ra cor-**TAR** may-**TAL**
Hoe	Azadón	ah-sa-**DON**
Hose	Manguera	man-**GAY**-rah
Knife	Navaja	na-**VA**-ha
Ladder	Escalera de mano	es-ka-**LAY**-rah day **MAN**-oh
Level	Nivel	**KNEE**-vell
Light	Luz	loose
Machine	Máquina	**MA**-key-nah

English	Español	Guide
Miter box	Caja de mitra	KA-ha day ME-tra
Mop	Trapeador	tra-pay-ah-DOOR
Nail	Clavo	CLAH-vo
Nut	Tuerca	too-AIR-ka
Paint	Pintura	peen-TOO-rah
Pan	Cacerola	ca-say-ROW-la
Pencil	Lápiz	LAH-pees
Pipe	Tubo	TOO-bow
Plane	Plano	PLA-no
Plaster	Yeso	YEA-so
Pick	Pico	P-co
Pliers	Alicates	al-lee-KA-tays
Plywood	Madera laminada	ma-DEAR-ah la-me-NA-da
Power saw	Serrucho eléctrico	say-ROO-cho ay-LEC-tree-co
Putty	Masilla	ma-SEE-ya
Rope	Cuerda	coo-AIR-da
Shovel	Pala	PA-la
Rock	Piedra	p-A-dra
Rebar	Varilla	bar-REE-ya
Ruler	Regla	RAY-gla
Rake	Rastrillo	ras-TREE-yo
Sand	Arena	ah-RAY-na
Sand paper	Papel de lija	pa-PEL day LEE-ha

English	Español	Guide
Saw	Serrucho	say-**ROO**-cho
	Sierra	see-**AIR**-rah
Scaffold	Andamio	an-da-**ME**-oh
Screwdriver	Destornillador	days-tor-knee-ya-**DOOR**
Screw	Tornillo	tore-**KNEE**-yo
Solder	Soldadura	sol-da-**DO**-rah
Soldering iron	Plancha de soldar	**PLAN**-cha day sol-**DAR**
Staple	Grapa	**GRA**-pa
Stapler	Engrapadora	en-gra-pa-**DOOR**-ah
Scissors	Tijeras	t-**HAIR**-ahs
Scraper	Raspador	ras-pa-**DOOR**
Shingle	Ripia	**REE**-p-ah
Stucco	Estuco	es-**STEW**-co
Stud	Tachón	ta-**CHON**
Tape	Cinta	**SEEN**-ta
Tape measure	Cinta para medir	**SEEN**-ta para may-**DEAR**
Tar	Brea	**BRAY**-ah
Tarpaper	Papel de brea	pa-**PEL** day **BRAY**-ah
Thinner	Diluyente	dee-loo-**YEN**-tay
Tile (roofing)	Teja	**TAY**-ha
Tile (decorative)	Cerámica	say-**RAM**-e-ka
Tool	Herramienta	air-rah-me-**N**-ta

English	Español	Guide
Trowel	Llana	YA-na
Trash can	Basurero	bah-sue-RARE-oh
Water	Agua	AH-goo-ah
Wedge	Cuña	COON-ya
Wheelbarrow	Caretilla	ca-ray-TEE-ya
Wood	Madera	ma-DAY-rah
Wire	Alambre	al-AHM-bray
Wire brush	Cepillo de alambre	say-P-yo day al-AHM-bray
Wrench	Llave de tuercas	YA-vay day too-AIR-cas
Vise	Tornillo de banco	torn-KNEE-yo day BAN-co

Framing — La Estructura

Construction terms can vary from country to country, and slang terms are as widely used in Latin America as they are in the United States. To help you work almost anywhere in Latin America, we have selected construction terms which are generic in Spanish. If there is a problem in communication, don't hesitate to ask this question: *¿Cómo se dice en español?* How do you say that in Spanish? Then, get ready to learn a new work, and don't forget to share the word's meaning in English with your co-worker.

English	Español	Guide
Beam	Viga	V-ga
Bearing wall	Pared de carga	pa-RED day CAR-ga
Ceiling joist	Viga de techo	V-ga day TAY-cho
Collar tie	Vigueta de amarre	v-GAY-ta day ah-MAR-ray
Cross bridging	Amarre	ah-MAR-ray
Floor joist	Viga de entre piso	V-ga day N-tray P-so
Girder	Viga principal	V-ga preen-see-PAL
Headset	Viga de cabecera	V-ga day ca-bay-SAY-rah
Plate	Viga horizontal	V-ga or-ee-son-TAL
Rafter	Viga	V-ga
Ridge board	Cumbrera	coom-BRAY-ra
Roof sheathing	Entablando de techo	n-ta-BLAN-doe day TAY-cho
Sill	Soporte	so-POR-tay
Steel studs	Montantes de acero	mon-TAN-tays day ah-SAY-row
Stud (wooden)	Montantes de madera	mon-TAN-tays day ma-DARE-rah
Sub floor	Subsuelo	soob-SWAY-low

English	Español	Guide
Truss	Armadura de cubierto	arm-ma-DOO-rah day coo-bee-AIR-toe
Wall	Pared	pa-RED
Wall sheathing	Entablado de muro	n-ta-BLAN-do day MOO-row

The Roof – El Techo

English	Español	Guide
Chute	Rampa	RAHM-pa
Fabric	Tela	TAY-la
Felt	Fieltro de techar	fee-L-tro
Flashing	Plancha de escurrimiento	PLAHN-cha day es-coo-ree-me-N-toe
Gutter	Canalón	ca-na-LOAN
Insulation	Aislamiento	ice-la-me-N-toe
Membrane	Membrana	mem-BRA-na
Metal Flashing	Plancha de escurrimiento metal	PLAHN-cha day es-coo-ree-me-N-toe may-TAL
Roof	Techo	TAY-cho
Roofing cement	Cemento plástico	say-MEN-toe PLAS-t-co

English	Español	Guide
Roofing felt	Tela para aislar el techo	TAY-la PA-rah ice-LAR l TAY-cho
Roofing nails	Clavos de techo	CLA-vos day TAY-cho
Sheet Metal	Hojalata	OH-ha LA-ta
Shingles	Ripias	REE-p-ahs
Slope	Ángulo de inclinación	AHN-goo-low day n-clee-na-see-ON
Waterproof	Impermeable	m-pear-me-AH-blay

Electricity - Electricidad

An electrician or *electricista* has an important and dangerous job. In this specialty good communication is critical. Nothing is more important than making sure each member of the crew is working safely and that parts of the project are up to code.

English	Español	Guide
Ammeter	Amperímetro	am-pear-REE-may-tro
Ampere	Amperio	am-PEAR-ree-oh
Anchors	Áncora	AHN-core-rah
Breaker Panel	Panel de rompedor	pa-NAIL day rom-pay-DOOR

English	Español	Guide
Bulb	Bombilla	bomb-**BEE**-ya
	Foco	**FO**-co
Ceiling fan	Ventilador de techo	ven-tee-la-**DOOR** day **TAY**-cho
Circuit breaker	Interruptor automático Cortacircuito	n-ter-roop-**TOR** ow-toe-**MA**-tee-co core-ta-sear-coo-**EE**-toe
Connector	Conector	co-neck-**TOR**
Copper	Cobre	**CO**-bray
Duct	Conducto porta cables	con-**DUKE**-toe **POR**-ta **CA**-blays
Exposed	Exponer	x-pone-**AIR**
Fixture	Artefacto	are-tay-**FAC**-toe
Fluorescent	Fluorescente	flew-oh-ray-**SEN**-tay
Fuse	Fusible	foo-**SEE**-blay
Ground	Tierra	tee-**AIR**-rah
Ground Clamp	Grampa	**GRAM**-pa
Heater	Calentador	ca-lent-ta-**DOOR**
Hot	Caliente	ca-lee-**N**-tay
Incandescent	Incandescente	n-can-days-**SENT**-tay
Line	Línea	**LEAN**-nay-ah
Live Wire	Alambre vivo	ah-**LAMB**-ray **VEE**-vo
Load	Carga	**CAR**-ga

English	Español	Guide
Neutral	Neutral	nay-oo-TRAL
Pipe Threader	Rosca de tubería	ROWS-ca day too-bear-REE-ah
Electricity	Electricidad	a-leck-tree-see-DAD
Receptacle	Receptáculo	ray-cep-TA-coo-low
Splice	Empalmar	em-pahl-MAR
Strip (Verb)	Desaforrar	day-sa-for-RARE
Switch	Interruptor	en-tay-roop-TOR
Thermostat	Termostato	tear-moe-STAT-oh
Transformer	Transformador	trans-for-ma-DOOR
Tube	Tubo	TOO-bow
Voltmeter	Voltímetro	vol-TEE-may-tro
Volts	Voltajes	vol-TA-heys
Watts	Vatios	VA-tee-ohs

Plumbers — Plomeros

English	Español	Guide
Auger	Barrena	bar-RAY-na
Basin	Pila	PEE-la
Bend	Curva	COOR-va
Bin	Depósito	day-POE-see-toe

English	Español	Guide
Crimper	Plegador de tubos	play-ga-**DOOR** day **TOO**-bows
Drain	Desagüe	des-**AH**-gway
To drain	desaguar	des-ah-**GUAR**
Drainage	Drenaje Desagüe	dran-**NA**-hey; des-**AH**-gway
Drain plug	Tapón de evacuación	ta-**PON** day a-va-coo-ah-see-**ON**
Drain area	Área colectora	**AH**-ray-ah co-lec-**TOR**-ah
Drain valve	Válvula purgadora de sedimentos	**VAL**-voo-la purr-ga-**DOOR**-ah day say-dee-**MEN**-toes
Drain hole	Orficio de purga	or-**FEE**-see-oh day **PURR**-ga
Drain pipe	Tubo de desagüe	**TWO**-bow day des-**AH**-gway
Drain system	Sistema de drenaje	sis-**TAY**-ma day dray-**NA**-hey
Drainage fittings	Accesorios drenables	ah-ces-**ROAR**-ree-ohs dran-**NA**-blays
Drip	Gotero	go-**TAY**-row
Drip pan	Recoge gotas	ray-**CO**-hay **GO**-tas
Drop (liquid)	Gota	**GO**-ta
Elbow	Codo	**CO**-doe
Faucet	Grifo	**GREE**-foe

English	Español	Guide
Fitting	Ajuste	ah-WHO-stay
Flange	Brida	BRIE-da
Flow	Flujo	FLEW-ho
Gauge	Véase	VAY-ah-say
Header	Travesaño	tra-vase-AN-yo
Lavatory	Lavabo	LA-va-bo
Main water	Agua principal	AH-gua preen-see-PAL
Main sewer	Cloaca principal	clo-AH-ca preen-see-PAL
Kitchen sink	Fregadero	fray-ga-DAY-row
Pedestal sink	Lavabo pedestal	la-VA-bow ped-day-STAL
Pipe	Tubo	TOO-bow
Plug	Tapón	ta-PON
Plumbing	Plomería	plo-may-REE-ah
Plumbing fixtures	Artefactos sanitarios	are-tay-FACT-toes san-knee-TAR-ree-ohs
Pressure	Presión	pres-see-ON
Pump	Bomba	BOM-baa
Ring	Anillo	an-KNEE-yo
Sewage	Agua negro	AH-gooah NAY-grow
Sewer	Albañal	al-BAN-yal
Sewer tap	Boca de admisión	BO-ca day add-me-see-ON
Shut off	Válvula de cierre	VAL-voo-la day see-AIR-ree

113

English	Español	Guide
Sleeve	Manguito	man-GEE-toe
Tee	Véase T	VA-ah-say tay
Toilet bowl	Cisterna	cease-TER-na
Toilet tank	Tanque de sanitario	TAN-kay day san-knee-TAR-ree-oh
Trap	Trampa	TRAM-pa
Trench	Zanja	SAN-ha
Trim	Contramarcos	con-tra-MAR-cos
Valve	Válvula	VAL-voo-la

Masonry

English	Español	Guide
¾ header	Ladrillo de tres cuartos de pared	la-DREE-yo day trays coo-ARE-toes day pa-RED
Arch	Arco	ARE-co
Brace	Riostra	ree-OH-stra
Brick	Ladrillo	la-DREE-yo
Brick hammer	Martillo de enladrillador	mar-T-yo day n-la-dree-la-DOOR
Brick laid on end	Ladrillos de testa	la-DREE-yos day TES-ta

114

English	Español	Guide
Bricklayer	Albañil	al-ban-**YEEL**
Brick up	Enladrillar	n-la-dree-**YAR**
Brick wall	Muro de ladrillos	**MOO**-row day la-**DREE**-yos
Cell	Célula	**SAY**-loo-la
Concrete brick	Ladrillo de concreto	la-**DREE**-yo day con-**CRAY**-toe
Course	Capa	**CA**-pa
Edger	Borde	**BORE**-day
Face brick	Ladrillo de fachada	la-**DREE**-yo day fa-**CHA**-da
Fire brick	Ladrillo de fuego	la-**DREE**-yo day foo-**A**-go
Float	Flotador	flow-ta-**DOOR**
Header	Ladrillo a tizón	la-**DREE**-yo ah t-**SEWN**
Hod	Cuezo	coo-**WAY**-so
Insulating brick	Ladrillo aislador	la-**DREE**-yo ice-la-**DOOR**
Mortar mixer	Mezclador de mortero	Mace-cla-**DOOR** day more-**TAY**-row
Mud	Lodo	**LO**-doe
Rebar	Varilla	var-**REE**-ya
Row / line	Hilera	e-**LAIR**-ah
Rowlock	Ladrillos a sardinel	la-**DREE**-yos ah sar-d-**NELL**
Sill	Umbral	oom-**BRAL**

English	Español	Guide
Smooth brick	Ladrillo liso	la-DREE-yo LEE-so
Soldier course	Hilera de ladrillos	e-LAIR-rah day la-DREE-yos
Stone	Piedra	p-A-dra
Stretcher	Ladrillo al hilo	la-DREE-yo al E-low

Masonry Verbs

English	Español	Guide
To...		
Caulk	Calafatear	ca-la-fa-tay-ARE
Clean	Limpiar	leem-p-ARE
Cut	Cortar	core-TAR
Drill	Perforar	pear-for-ARE
Grout	Inyectar lechada	en-yec-TAR lay-CHA-da
Lay	Enladrillar	n-la-dree-YAR
Mix	Mezclar	mess-CLAR
Pour	Colar	co-LAR
Scrape	Raspar	rahs-PAR
Set up (dry)	Secar	say-CAR
Stack	Apilar	ah-p-LAR
Stop	Parar	pa-RAR

Safety Is Number One

Working inside the US or in another country, construction safety is a major concern. Safety practices in Latin America are quite different than they are in the US, and they vary from country to country. Most countries in Latin America have no construction safety regulatory agency like OSHA to oversee building practices. Use these terms to work safely, because in some Latin American countries safety rules are almost nonexistent!

English	Español	Guide
Accident	Accidente	ax-see-**DENT**-tay
Be careful.	Tenga cuidado.	**TEN**-gah kwee-**DA**-doe
Danger!	¡Peligro!	pay-**LEE**-grow
Electrocution	Electrocución	a-lec-tro-cue-see-**ON**
Excavation	Excavación	x-ka-vah-see-**ON**
Fall	Caída	ca-**EE**-da
Fire	Fuego	foo-**A**-go
Fire extinguisher	Extinguidor de fuego	x-ting-gee-**DOR** day foo-**A**-go
First aid	Primeros auxilios	pre-**MAY**-rows aux-**E**-lee-ohs
Guardrail	Barandillas	ba-ran-**DEE**-yas
Hard hat	Casco	**KAS**-co
Harness	Arnés	are-**NES**
Heat exhaustion	Agotamiento de calor	ah-go-ta-me-**N**-toe day ca-**LORE**

English	Español	Guide
High voltage	Alto voltaje	**AL**-toe vowl-**TA**-hey
Lifting	Levantamiento	lay-van-ta-me-**N**-toe
No smoking.	No fumar	no foo-**MAR**
Platform	Plataforma	pla-ta-**FOR**-ma
Protection	Protección	pro-teck-see-**ON**
Pulling nails	Sacando clavos	sa-**CAN**-doe **CLA**-vows
Safety belt	Cinturón de seguridad	seen-to-**RON** day say-goo-ree-**DAD**
Safety glasses	Anteojos de seguridad	anti-**OH**-hos day say-goo-ree-**DAD**
	Gafas de protección	**GA**-fas day pro-tec-see-**ON**
Scaffold	Andamio	an-da-**ME**-oh
Trench	Zanjas	**SAN**-has

One for the Road: Phrases to Use Any Time

Obviously, conversation is made up of more than just lists of words. It will take practice and determination for you to achieve free-flowing conversation. Learning Spanish is a slow and steady process for adults. It could take several months before you begin to "think" in Spanish, so don't expect to achieve native speaker speed over night! There will be times when you feel like you can't remember anything you've studied. That's natural. It happens to everyone. Don't be discouraged. The rewards you'll receive from learning to speak

Spanish are far greater than a little frustration. If you keep working, it won't be long before you'll have a break-through.

I think learning to speak Spanish is a lot like eating a great steak. You don't want to rush it. Cut each bite of your Spanish, and chew it carefully. Savor each morsel. Moving at a slower pace will help you retain what you learn longer—and you'll enjoy the process much more. After all, if you are going to take the time to learn a language that is as important as Spanish, why not make the process fun?

Spanish is a language that loaded with zest and flair. It is punctuated with single words and short phrases that really express a lot of sentiment. The next time you have an opportunity to observe native speakers, listen carefully. You may hear them switch from English to Spanish, depending on what they are saying. And, you might hear them use any of the "one-liners" listed below. Use the following list to help you take your conversational skills to the next level.

English	Español	Guide
Are you sure?	¿Está seguro? (a)	es-**TA** say-**GOO**-row
Excellent	Excelente	x-say-**LENT**-tay
Fantastic	Fantástico	fan-**TA**-stee-co
God bless you	Dios te bendiga	d-**OS** tay ben-**D**-ga
Good idea.	Buena idea.	boo-**A**-na e-**DAY**-ah

English	Español	Guide
Happy birthday	Feliz cumpleaños	fay-**LEASE** coom-play-**AHN**-yos
Have a nice day	Tenga un buen día	**TEN**-ga un boo-**WAYNE** **DEE**-ah
I agree	De acuerdo	day ah-coo-**AIR**-doe
I believe so	Creo que sí	**CRAY**-oh kay **SEE**
I'm so glad	Me alegro	may ah-**LAY**-gro
I'll be right back	Ahora vengo	ah-**OR**-ah **VEIN**-go
I'm leaving now	Ya me voy	ya may **VOY**
That's OK	Está bien	es-**TA** b-**N**
It's important	Es importante	es eem-pour-**TAHN**-tay
It's serious.	Es grave.	es **GRA**-vay
It's possible.	Es posible	es po-**SEE**-blay
Maybe.	Quizás.	key-**SAHS**
Me, neither	Yo tampoco.	yo tam-**PO**-co
Me, too	Yo también.	yo tam-b-**N**
More or less	Más o menos.	mas oh **MAY**-nos
Really?	¿De veras?	day **VER**-ahs
Sure	¡Claro!	**CLA**-row
That depends.	Depende.	day-**PEN**-day
We'll see you.	Nos vemos.	nos **VAY**-mos

English Spanish Dictionary

A

Abdomen = Abdomen
Above = Encima
Abscess = Absceso
Accident = Accidente
Address = Dirección
Adorable = Adorable
Afraid of = Miedo de
After meals = Después de las comidas
Age = Edad
Airline = Aerolínea
Airplane = Avión
Airport = Aeropuerto
Aisle (church) = Nave lateral
Aisle = Pasillo
Allergy = Alergia
Altar = Altar
Ammeter = Amperímetro
Analgesic = Analgésico
Anchors = Áncora
Anemia = Anemia
Anesthetic = Anestésico
Angel = Ángel
Animal = Animale
Ankle = Tobillo
Antacid = Antiácido
Antibiotic = Antibiótico
Anticoagulant = Anticoagulante
Antidote = Antídoto
Antihistamine = Antihistamínicos
Anti-inflammatory = Anti-inflamatorio
Antiseptic = Antiséptico
Anus = Ano
Anxiety = Ansiedad
Apostle = Apóstol
Appendicitis = Apendicitis
Appendix = Apéndice
Apple = Manzana
Apply = Aplique
April = Abril

Apse = Ábside
Arch = Arco
Archbishop = Arzobispo
Are you sure? = ¿Está seguro? (a)
Arm = Brazo
Arrival = Llegada
Arthritis = Artritis
As directed by your doctor = Según las instrucciones de su doctor.
Ashamed = Vergüenza
Aspirin = Aspirina
Asthma = Asma
Astringent = Astringente
At bedtime = A la hora de acostarse
Attic fan = Ventilador de ático
Auger = Barrena
August = Agosto
Aunt = Tía
Avenue = Avenida
Avocado = Aguacate
Ax = Hacha

B

Back = Espalda
Bad = Mal
Bad reaction = Mala reacción
Bag = Bolsa
Bakery = Panadería
Balloon = Globo
Banana = Plátano
Bank = Banco
Baptismal font = Pila bautismal
Barber shop = Peluquería
Barbiturate = Barbitúrico
Barrage claim = Reclamo de equipaje
Barrel = Barril
Basin = Pila
Bathing suit = Traje de baño

Bathroom = Baño, Servicio
Be careful. = Tenga cuidado.
Beach = Playa
Beam = Viga
Bearing wall = Pared de carga
Beauty salon = Salón de belleza
Beef = Carne de vaca
Beer = Cerveza
Before meals = Antes de las comidas
Behind = Detrás
Bell = Campana
Belt = Cinturón
Bend = Curva
Beside = Al lado de
Between meals = Entre las comidas
Beverage = Bebida
Bible = Biblia
Big = Grande
Bin = Depósito
Birds = Pájaros
Bishop = Obispo
Black = Negro
Black beans = Frijoles negros
Blasphemy = Blasfemia
Bleeding = Sangrado
Blessing = Bendición
Blister = Ampolla
Blocks = Bloques de madera
Blood = Sangre
Blue = Azul
Board = Tabla de madera
Body = Cuerpo
Bolts = Pernos
Books = Libros
Boots = Botas
Box = Caja
Brace = Riostra
Brain = Cerebro
Bread = Pan
Breaker Panel = Panel de rompedores

Breakfast = Desayuno
Breathe deeply. = Respire profundo.
Brick = Ladrillo
Brick hammer = Martillo de enladrillador
Brick laid on edge = Ladrillos a canto
Brick laid on end = Ladrillos de testa
Brick up = Enladrillar
Bride = Novia
Bridesmaid = Dama de honor
Bring me that. = Tráigame eso
Broccoli = Brócoli
Broken bone = Hueso roto
Bronchitis = Bronquitis
Broom = Escoba
Brother = Hermano
Brother-in-law = Cuñado
Brown = Moreno
Bruise = Contusión
Brush (paint) = Brocha
Bucket = Cubo
Bulb = Bombilla, Foco
Bump = Hinchazón
Burn = Quemadura
Burning pain = Dolor quemante
Bus = Autobús
Bus station = Estación de autobuses
Butter = Mantequilla

C
Cable = Cable
Cake = Pastel, Queque
Calm = Tranquilo
Calm down. = Cálmese
Can = Lata
Cancer = Cáncer
Candy = Dulce
Canine tooth = Diente canino

Cantaloupe = Melón,
Cantalupo
Canvas = Lona
Capsule = Cápsula
Car = Carro
Cards = Cartas
Carol = Villancico
Carrot = Zanahoria
Carry this = Lleve esto.
Carry on baggage =
Equipaje de mano
Cassock = Sotana
Cathedral = Catedral
Cat = Gato
Cauliflower = Coliflor
Caulk = Sellador
Caulk gun = Pistola de
sellador
Ceiling = Techo
Ceiling Fan = Ventilador
de techo
Ceiling joist = Viga de
techo
Celery = Apio
Cement block =
Bloque de cemento
Cereal = Cereal
Chalice = Cáliz
Chapel = Capilla
Chaplain = Capellán
Chapter = Capítulo
Charity = Caridad
Chaulk line = Línea de
tiza
Checkers = Juego de
damas
Cheese = Queso
Chemotherapy =
Quimioterapia
Chest = Pecho
Chewing gum = Chicle
Chicken = Pollo
Chicken pox = Varicela
Chicken wire =
Alambrada
Child = Niño *(a)*
Chills = Escalofrío
Chin = Barbilla
Chips = Tostaditas

Chisel = Cincel
Chocolate = Chocolate
Choir = Coro
Choir director = Director
del coro
Choir Loft = Coro
Christ = Cristo
Church = Iglesia
Chute = Rampa
Circuit Breaker =
Interruptor automático,
Cortacircuito
City hall = Municipio
Clamp = Pinza
Clean = Limpiar
Close = Cierre
Cloth = Trapo
Coconut = Coco
Codeine = Codeína
Coffee = Café
Cold = Frío
Cold = Frío.
Cold = Catarro
Cold weather = Hace frío
Collar tie = Vigueta de
amarre
Colon = Colón
Coloring/painting = Pintar
Come here = Venga aquí.
Compressor = Compresor
Concrete = Concreto
Concrete brick = Ladrillo
de concreto
Conduit (cable) =
Conducto de cable
Conduit (pipe) =
Conducto, Tubo
Confession = Confesión
Confirmation =
Confirmación
Congregation = Fieles
Connector = Conector
Consecrated wafer =
Hostia
Constant pain = Dolor
constante
Constipation =
Estreñimiento

Contraceptive = Contraceptivo
Convent = Convento
Cookie = Galleta
Cool = Hace fresco
Corn = Maíz
Corrugated metal = Metal corrugado
Cortisone = Cortisona
Cough = Tos
Cough drop = Pastillas para la tos
Cough syrup = Jarabe para la tos
Course = Capa
Cousin = Primo *(a)*
Cracker = Galleta salada
Cramp = Calambre
Crayon = Lápics de color
Cream = Crema
Cream = Crema
Crimper = Plegador de tubos
Cross = Cruz
Cross bridging = Amarre
Crowbar = Barra
Cucumber = Pepino
Cup = Una copa
Custard = Flan
Customs = Aduana
Cut = Cortar *(v)*
Cute = Mono
Cutter = Cortador
Cymbals = Platillos

D

Danger= Peligro
Dark = Oscuro
Date of birth = Fecha de nacimiento
Daughter = Hija
Daughter-in-law = Nuera
Deacon = Diácono
Decaffeinated coffee = Café descafeinado
December = diciembre
Decreased appetite = Disminución del apetito

Deep pain = Dolor profundo
Departure/Exit/Gate = Salida
Depth = Profundidad
Dessert = Postre
Destination = Destinación
Devil = Diablo
Diabetes = Diabetes
Diaphragm = Diafragma
Diarrhea = Diarrea
Diet soda = Refresco dieta
Dimensional lumber = Barrote dimensional
Dinner = Cena
Disciple = Discípulo
Disinfectant = Desinfectante
Diuretic = Diurético
Dizziness = Mareos, Vértigo
Do you like….? = ¿Te gusta….?
Do you speak English? = ¿Habla inglés?
Do you understand? = ¿Comprende?
Dogs = Perros
Dolls = Muñecas
Dowel = Taco, Clavija
Down = Abajo
Downspout = Bajada de aguas
Drain = Desagüe
Drain area = Área colectora
Drain hole = Orificio de purga
Drain pipe = Tubo de desagüe
Drain plug = Tapón de evacuación
Drain system = Sistema de drenaje
Drain valve = Válvula purgadora de sedimentos
Drainage = Drenaje, Desagüe

Drainage fittings =
Accesorios de drenaje
Drawing = Dibujando
Dress = Vestido
Dried Beans = Frijoles
Drill = Barrena, Taladro
Drill = Perforar
Drill bit = Broca
Drip = Gotero
Drip pan = Recoge gotas
Drop = Una gota
Drop (liquid) = Gota
Drum = Tambor
Dry mouth = Boca seca
Duct = Conducto porta
cables

E
Ear = Oreja
East = Este
Edge = Borde
Edge strips = Tira de
borde
Edger = Borde
Egg = Huevo
Elbow = Codo
Electric cord = Extensión
eléctrica
Electrocution =
Electrocución
Epoxy putty = Masilla
epóxica
Esophagus = Esófago
Eternal = Eterno
Evangelist = Evangelista
Excavation = Excavación
Excellent = Excelente
Excellent = Excelente
Excuse me. = ¡Perdón!
Exposed = Exponer
Extension cord = Cable
de extensión
Exterior = Exterior
Externally =
Externamente
Eye = Ojo

F
Fabric = Tela
Face = Cara
Face brick = Ladrillo de
fachada
Falls = Caídas
Fantastic = Fantástico
Far = Lejos
Father = Padre
Father-in-law = Suegro
Faucet = Grifo
February = febrero
Felt = Fieltro de techar
Fever = Fiebre
Fever = Fiebre
File = Lima
Fine = Muy bien.
Finger = Dedo
Finish – smooth =
Acabado liso
Finish (rough) = Acabado
ordinario
Finish (wood) = Acabado
Fire = Fuego
Fire brick = Ladrillo de
fuego
Fire department =
Departamento de
bomberos
Fire extinguisher =
Extinguidor de fuego
First aid = Primeros
auxilios
First communion =
Primera comunión
First name = Primer
nombre
Fish = Pez
Fish = Pescado
Fitting = Ajuste
Fixture = Artefacto
Flange = Brida
Flashing = Plancha de
escurrimiento
Flight = Vuelto
Float = Flotador
Floor = Piso
Floor joist = Viga de entre
piso

Florist = Florería
Flow = Flujo
Flowers = Flores
Flu = Influenza
Fluorescent light = Luz fluorescente
Flute = Flauta
Font = Pila
Foot = Pie
For external use = Para uso externo
Forever = Siempre
Foundation = Fundación
Fractures = Fracturas
Framing = Estructura
Friday = viernes
Fruit = Fruta
Full name = Nombre completo
Funny = Chistoso
Fuse = Fusible

G
Gall bladder = Vesícula billar
Gall stones = Cálculos en la vesícula
Games = Juegos
Gas station = Gasolinera
Gauge = Véase
Get undressed. = Desvístase
Get up = Súbase
Get up on the table. = Súbase a la mesa.
Girder = Viga principal
Give it to me. = Démelo
Glaucoma = Glaucoma
Gloves = Guantes
Glue = Goma
Glue gun = Pistola de pegamento
God = Dios, Señor
God bless you = Dios te bendiga
Godfather = Padrino
Godmother = Madrina
Good = Bueno

Good afternoon = Buenas tardes
Good idea. = Buena idea.
Good morning = Buenos días
Good night = Buenas noches.
Good = Bien
Good-bye = Adiós
Gospel = Evangelio
Grain = Veta
Gram = Gramo
Granddaughter = Nieta
Grandfather = Abuelo
Grandmother = Abuela
Grandson = Nieto
Grape = Uva
Grapefruit = Toronja
Gravel = Grava
Gray = Gris
Green = Verde
Green bean = Ejote
Green bell pepper = Pimiento verde
Green peas = Guisantes
Grocery store = Grosería
Groom = Novio
Ground = Tierra
Ground Clamp = Grampa
Ground Rod = Barra de tierra
Grout = Lechada
Grout (v)= Inyectar lechada
Guardrail = Barandillas
Guitar = Guitarra
Gums = Encías
Gutter = Canalón
Gypsum = Yeso

H
Hack saw = Sierra para cortar metal
Half = Una media
Half = Medio
Half and half = Leche con crema
Halo = Aureola

Ham = Jamón
Hamburger = Hamburguesa
Hammer = Martillo
Hand = Mano
Handsome = Guapo
Happy birthday = Feliz cumpleaños
Hard hat = Casco
Hard palate = Paladar duro
Hard wood = Madera dura
Hard-boiled egg = Huevo duro
Hardware = Cerrajería
Harness = Arnés
Hat = Sombrero
Have a nice day = Tenga un buen día
Hay fever = Fiebre de heno
He = Él
Head = Cabeza
Headache = Dolor de cabeza
Header = Travesaño
Headset = Viga de cabecera
Heart = Corazón
Heart = Corazón
Heart = Corazón
Heat exhaustion = Agotamiento de calor
Heater = Calentador
Heaven = Cielo
Height = Altura
Hell = Infierno
Help him. = Ayúdelo
Help me. = Ayúdeme
Hepatitis = Hepatitis
Here = Aquí
Heresy = Herejía
Heretic = Hereje
Herpes = Herpes
Hi = ¡Hola!
High blood pressure = Presión sanguínea alta

High voltage = Alto voltaje
His, her or Your *(polite)* = Su, Sus
Hives = Urticaria
Hives = Ronchas de la piel
Hod = Cuezo
Hoe = Azadón
Hole = Perforación
Hole Cutter = Cortador de perforación
Holiness = Santidad
Holy Spirit = Espíritu Santo
Holy Water = Agua bendito
Home telephone number = Número de teléfono de su casa
Honey = Miel
Horse = Caballo
Hose = Manguera
Hospital = Hospital
Hot = Caliente, Calor
Hot Dog = Perro caliente
Hot weather = Hace calor
Hotel = Hotel
How are you = ¿Cómo está?
How do you say it in Spanish = ¿Cómo se dice en español?
How many = ¿Cuántos?
How much = ¿Cuánto?
How old are you = ¿Cuántos años tienes?
How = ¿Cómo?
Hungry = Hambre
Husband = Esposo
Hymn book = Himnario
Hypoglycemia = Hipoglucemia

I
I = Yo
I agree = De acuerdo
I believe so = Creo que sí

I don't understand. = No comprendo.
I respect you. = Le respeto.
I speak a little Spanish. = Hablo poco español.
I'm so glad = Me alegro
Ice cream = Helado
I'll be right back = Ahora vengo
I'm leaving now = Ya me voy
In front of = En frente de
In the afternoon = Por la tarde
In the evening = Por la noche
In the morning = Por la mañana
Incandescent = Incandescente
Incense = Incienso
Incisor = Diente incisivo
Increased appetite = Aumento del apetito
Indigestion = Indigestión
Inhaler = Inhalador
Inside = Adentro
Insomnia = Insomnio
Insulating brick = Ladrillo aislador
Insulation = Aislamiento
Insulin = Insulina
Interior = Interior
Intermittent pain = Dolor intermitente
Iron = Hierro
It's important = Es importante
It's serious. = Es grave.
Itching = Picazón
It's possible. = Es posible

J
Jacket = Chaqueta
Jam = Mermelada
Jamb brick = Ladrillo de jamba

January = enero
Jaundice = Ictericia
Jeans = Jeans, Vaqueros
Jesus = Jesús
Jewelry store = Joyería
Joiner = Carpintero
Joint compound = Masa de yeso
Jointer = Escarbador de juntas
Jokes = Chistes
Juice = Jugo
July = julio
Jump rope = Cuerda para brincar
June = junio
Jungle = Selva

K
Keep refrigerated. = Guarda en el refrigerador.
Kidney = Riñón
Kidney stones = Cálculos en los riñones
Kilo = Kilo
Kitchen sink = Fregadero
Knee = Rodilla
Knife = Navaja

L
Ladder = Escalera de mano
Lard = Manteca
Large intestine = Intestino grueso
Laryngitis = Laringitis
Last name (surname) = Apellido
Later. = Más tarde.
Laundromat = Lavandería
Lavatory = Lavabo
Laxative = Laxante
Lay = Enladrillar
Leader = Líder
Lectern = Atril
Leg = Pierna

Lemon = Limón
Length = Largo
Less = Menos
Let's go. = Vámonos
Lettuce = Lechuga
Leukemia = Leucemia
Level = Nivel
Library = Biblioteca
Lie down. = Acuéstese.
Lifting = Levantamiento
Light = Claro
Light = Luz
Like this = Así
Like this? = ¿Así?
Lime = Lima
Line = Línea
Liniment = Linimento
Linoleum = Linóleo
Liter = Litro
Little = Pequeño
Live Wire = Alambre vivo
Liver = Hígado
Load = Carga
Lost and found = Oficina
de objetos perdidos
Lotion = Loción
Love = Amor
Low blood pressure =
Presión sanguínea baja
Lozenge = Pastilla
Lubricant = Lubricante
Lumber = Madera de
construcción
Lump = Bulto
Lunch = Almuerzo
Lung = Pulmón

M
Machine = Máquina
Main sewer = Cloaca
principal
Main water = Agua
principal
Mallet = Mazo
Mango = Mango
Marble = Mármol
March = Marzo
Market = Mercado

Mass = Misa
Mastic = Mastique
Maternal surname =
Apellido materno
May = Mayo
Maybe = Quizás.
Me neither = Yo tampoco.
Me too = Yo también.
Meal or food = Comida
Measles = Sarampión
Meat = Carne
Membrane = Membrana
Middle name = Segundo
nombre
Migraine = Jaqueca,
Migraña
Mild pain = Dolor
moderado
Mildew = Moho
Milk = Leche
Milliliter = Mililitro
Minister = Ministro
Miracle = Milagro
Miss = Señorita
Mission trip = Viaje de
misión
Miter box = Caja de mitra
Mix = Mezclar
Molar = Muela, Molar
Monastery = Monasterio
Monday = lunes
Money exchange =
Cambio
Monk = Monje
Mop = Trapeador
More = Más
More or less = Más o
menos.
Morphine = Morfina
Mortar mixer = Mezclador
de mortero
Mother = Madre
Mother-in-law = Suegra
Mountains = Montañas
Mouth = Boca
Move that here. = Mueve
eso aquí
Movie theatre = Cine
Mrs. or Ma'am = Señora

Mud = Lodo
Mumps = Paperas
Museum = Museo
Mushroom = Champiñón
Music = Música
My = Mi, Mis
My name is = Me llamo

N
Nail = Uña
Nail gun = Pistola de
clavos, Pistola
Nails = Clavos
Name of child = Nombre
de niño
Name of husband/wife =
Nombre de esposo (a)
Narcotic = Narcótico
Nationality =
Nacionalidad
Nave = Nave
Near = Cerca de
Neck = Cuello
Neck brick = Ladrillo de
cuello
Neutral = Neutral
New = Nuevo
Nice = Simpático
Nice to meet you =
¡Mucho gusto!
Nice weather = Hace
buen tiempo
Nitroglycerine =
Nitroglicerina
No smoking. = No fumar
Non-believer = Pagano
Non-fat milk = Leche sin
grasa
North = Norte
Nose = Nariz
Not like this = Así no
November = noviembre
Now = Ahora
Nun = Monja
Nuts = Tuercas

O
October = octubre
Offering = Oferta
Offertory = Ofertorio
Old = Viejo
Omelet = Tortilla de
huevos
On an empty stomach =
Con el estómago vacío.
One tablespoon = Una
cucharada
One teaspoon = Una
cucharadita
Onion = Cebolla
Only when necessary =
Solo cuando es necesario
Only when you have pain
= Solo cuando tiene dolor
Open = Abra
Open your mouth. =
Abre la boca.
Orange = Naranja
Our = Nuestro (-os),
Nuestra (-as)
Outside = Afuera
Over there = Allá
Overcoat = Abrigo

P
Pain = Dolor
Paint = Pintura
Pajamas = Pijamas
Pan = Cacerola
Paneling = Paneles
Pants = Pantalones
Papaya = Papaya
Parable = Parábola
Parish = Parroquia
Park = Parque
Party = Fiesta
Pastor = Pastor (n)
Patch = Parche
Paternal surname =
Apellido paterno
Peach = Melocotón
Peanut butter = Crema de
cacahuate

Pear = Pera
Pedestal sink = Lavabo
pedestal
Pencil = Lápiz
Penicillin = Penicilina
Pew = Banco
Pharmacy = Farmacia
Pick = Pico
Pick up all these. =
Recoja todo estos
Pie = Tarta
Piety = Piedad
Pilgrim = Peregrino
Pill = Píldora
Pineapple = Piña
Pink = Rosa
Pious = Piadoso
Pipe = Tubo
Pipe Threader = Rosca
de tubería
Place of birth = Lugar de
nacimiento
Plane = Plano
Plank = Tablón
Plaster = Yeso
Plaster = Yeso
Plate = Viga horizontal
Platform = Plataforma
Playing music = Tocando
música
Please! = ¡Por favor!
Pliers = Alicates
Plug = Tapón
Plumber = Plomero
Plumbing = Plomería
Plumbing fixtures =
Artefactos sanitarios
Plywood = Madera
laminada
Pneumonia = Pulmonía
Point to it. = Indíquelo
Police station = Estación
de policía
Pope = Papa
Porch = Pórtico
Pork chop = Chuleta de
puerco
Post office = Correo
Potato = Patata

Pound = Libra
Pour = Colar
Power = Electricidad
Power saw = Serrucho
eléctrico
Prayer = Oración
Precast = Hormigón en
bloques
Precious = Precioso
Prescription = Receta
médica, Fórmula, Receta
Pressure = Presión
Pretty = Bonita
Priest = Cura
Primer = Base
Propane = Propano
Propane = Propano
Protection = Protección
Psalm = Salmo
Pudding = Pudín
Pulling nails = Sacando
clavos
Pulpit = Púlpito
Pump = Bomba
Pumpkin = Calabaza
Purple = Morado
Put it there. = Póngalo allí
Putty = Masilla, Mástique
Putty knife = Espátula
angosta
Puzzles =
Rompecabezas

R
Rafter = Viga
Rain = Lluvia
Raincoat = Impermeable
Raisin = Pasita
Rake = Rastrillo
Rash = Erupción
Reading = Leyendo
Really? = ¿De veras?
Rebar = Varilla
Receptacle =
Receptáculo, Caja de
contacto
Rectum = Recto
Red = Rojo

Red wine = Vino tinto
Reinforce = Reforzado
Remove these. = Quite estos
Repeat please. = Repita por favor.
Reservation = Reserva
Resin = Resina
Restaurant = Restaurante
Restless = Inquieto
Rice = Arroz
Ridge board = Cumbrera
Right = Razón
Ring = Anillo
Robe = Bata
Rock = Piedra
Roll = Rollo
Roof sheathing = Entablando de techo
Rope = Cuerda
Rosary = Rosario
Round = Redondo
Row = Fila
Row = Hilera
Rowlock = Ladrillos a sardinel
Ruler = Regla

S
Safe = Seguro
Safety belt = Cinturón de seguridad
Safety glasses = Anteojos de seguridad, Gafas de protección
Saint = Santo, Santa
Salad = Ensalada
Sanctuary = Santuario
Sand = Arena
Sand paper = Papel de lija
Sandals = Sandalias
Sander = Lijadora
Sandwich = Sándwich
Saturday = sábado
Sausage = Salchicha
Saw = Serrucho, Sierra

Saw blade = Hoja de sierra
Sawn timber = Madera aserradas
Scaffold = Andamio
Scaffold = Andamio
Scarf = Bufanda
School = La escuela
School = Escuela
Scissors = Tijeras
Scrambled egg = Huevo revuelto
Scrape = Raspar
Scraped = Raspadas
Scraper = Raspador
Screwdriver = Destornillador
Screwdriver (*Phillips*) = Destornillador de cruz
Screws = Tornillos
Seafood = Mariscos
Seat = Asiento
Security = Seguridad
Sedative = Sedante
September = Septiembre
Sermon = Sermón
Service = Servicio
Set up (dry) = Secar
Severe pain = Dolor fuerte
Sewage = Agua negro
Sewer = Albañal
Sewer tap = Boca de admisión
Shake well. = Agítese bien.
She = Ella
Sheeting = Lámina
Shingle = Ripia
Shirt = Camisa
Shoe store = Zapatería
Shoes = Zapatos
Shorts = Pantalones cortos
Shoulder = Hombro
Shovel = Pala
Show me. = Indícalo.

132

Shut off = Válvula de cierre, Válvula de interrupción
Shy = Tímido
Sidewalk = Banqueta
Silicone = Silicón
Silicone sealant = Sellador de silicón
Sill = Umbral
Sin = Pecado
Sir or Mister = Señor
Sister = Hermana
Sister-in-law = Cuñada
Sit down = Siéntese
Skin = Piel
Skirt = Falda
Slab = Losa
Slate = Pizarra
Sledgehammer = Marro
Sleepiness = Sueño
Sleepy = Sueño
Sleeve = Manguito
Slope = Inclinación
Small intestine = Intestino delgado
Smooth = Liso
Smooth brick = Ladrillo liso
Snack = Merienda
Sneakers = Tenis
So so = Así así
Socks = Calcetines
Soft drink = Refresco, Soda
Soft palate = Paladar blando
Solder = Soldadura
Soldering iron = Plancha de soldar
Soldier course = Hilera de ladrillos
Solution = Solución
Son = Hijo
Songs = Canciones
Son-in-law = Yerno
Soup = Sopa
Sour cream = Crema de leche agria
South = Sur

Spackle = Junta de cemento
Sparingly = Poquito
Speak more slowly. = Habla más despacio
Spine = Espina
Splice = Empalmar
Sports = Deportes
Sprain = Torcedura
Spray paint gun = Pistola de pintar
Squash = Calabacera
Stack = Apilar
Stain = Tinta
Stained glass = Vidriera
Stand up = Levántese
Stapler = Engrapadora
Staples = Grapas
Steak = Bistec
Steel studs = Montantes de acero
Steeple = Campanario
Steroid = Esteroide
Stomach = Estómago
Stone = Piedra
Stop = Parar
Store = Tienda
Story = Cuento
Straight ahead = Adelante
Strained = Distendidas
Strawberry = Fresa
Street = Calle
Stretcher = Ladrillo al hilo
Strip (V) = Desaforrar
Stucco = Estuco
Stud = Tachón
Stud (wooden) = Montantes de madera
Stuffed animal = Animale de peluche
Sub floor = Subsuelo
Subway = Metro
Suit = Traje
Sunday = Domingo
Sunny weather = Hace sol
Super market = Super Mercado

Suppositories = Supositorios
Sure = ¡Claro!
Sweater = Suéter
Sweet potato = Camote
Swelling = Inflamación
Switch = Interruptor

T

Tablet = Tableta
Take = Toma
Take a deep breath. = Aspire profundo.
Take the medicine = Toma la medicina
Tamarind = Tamarindo
Tape = Cinta
Tape measure = Cinta para medir
Tar = Brea
Tarpaper = Papel de brea
Taxi = Taxi
Tea = Té
Tee = Véase T
Teeth = Dientes
Tell me= Dime
Terminal = Terminal
Thank you. = Gracias.
Thanks for your patience = Gracias por su paciencia
That = Ese, Esa
That depends= Depende.
That one over there = Aquel, Aquellos, Aquella, Aquellas
That's OK = Está bien
The *(Singular)* = El (m), La (f)
The pleasure is mine = El gusto es mío
Theatre = Teatro
Theology = Teología
There = Allí
Thermostat = Termostato
These = Estos, Estas
They = Ellos, Ellas *(f)*
Thinner = Diluyente

Thirsty = Sed
This = Este, Esta
Those = Esos, Esas
Throat = Garganta
Throbbing pain = Dolor pulsante
Thursday = jueves
Ticket = Boleto
Tie = Corbata
Tile = Cerámica *(decorative)*
Tile = Teja *(roofing)*
To accept = Aceptar
To affected areas = En los áreas afectados
To ask = Preguntar
To baptize = Bautizar
To call = Llamar
To carry = Llevar
To drain = Desaguar
To help = Ayudar
To kneel = Arrodillarse
To lift = Levantar
To need = Necesitar
To play = Jugar
To pray = Rezar
To preach = Predicar
To prepare = Preparar
To rain = Llover
To return = Regresar
To sing = Cantar
To the left = A la izquierda
To the right = A la derecha
To use = Usar
To work = Trabajar
To worship = Adorar
Toe = Dedo del pie
Toilet bowl = Cisterna
Toilet tank = Tanque de sanitario
Tomato = Tomate
Tongue = Lengua
Tonsil = Amígdala
Tool = Herramienta
Tooth = Diente
Torch (propane) = Antorcha de propano

134

Toys = Juguetes
Train station = Estación de tren
Train station = Estación de tren
Tranquilizers = Tranquilizantes
Transept = Crucero
Transformer = Transformador
Transportation = Transportación
Trap = Trampa
Trash can = Basurero
Trench = Zanja
Trim = Contramarcos
Trowel = Llana
Truss = Armadura de cubierto
T-shirt = Camiseta
Tube = Tubo
Tuberculosis = Tuberculosis
Tuesday = Martes
Tuna = Atún
Turkey = Pavo
Turn = Doble
Turn around. = Voltéese
Turtle = Tortuga

U
Umbrella = Paraguas
Uncle = Tío
Under = Debajo
Underwear = Ropa interior
Up = Arriba
Uvula = Úvula

V
Vaccine = Vacuna
Valve = Válvula
Varnish = Barniz
Vegetables = Vegetales
Veneer = Chapado

Vent = Orificio de ventilación
Verse = Verso
Very good! = ¡Muy bien!
Very important! = Muy importante!
Vest = Chaleco
Vestibule = Vestíbulo
Vestments = Vestiduras
Vestry = Sacristía
Vise = Tornillo de banco
Vitamins = Vitaminas
Voltmeter = Voltímetro
Volts = Voltajes
Vows = Promesas solemnes

W
Wait = Espere
Wall = Pared
Wall sheathing = Entablado de muro
Walnut = Nogal
Water = Agua
Water Heater = Calentador de agua
Watermelon = Sandía
Waterproof = Impermeable
Watts = Vatios
We = Nosotros, Nosotras (f)
We'll see you. = Nos vemos.
Wedge. = Cuña
Wednesday = miércoles
Weight gain = Aumento de peso
West = Oeste
What? = ¿Qué?
What's happening? = ¿Qué pasa?
What's the weather? = ¿Qué tiempo hace?
What's your name? = ¿Cómo se llama?
Wheelbarrow = Caretilla
When? = ¿Cuándo?

135

Where are you from? =
¿De dónde es?
Where do you live? =
¿Dónde vives?
Where is...? = ¿Dónde
está?
Where? = ¿Dónde?
Which? = ¿Cuál?
White = Blanco
White wine = Vino blanco
Who? = ¿Quién?
Why? = ¿Por qué?
Wife = Esposa
Window = Ventana
Windy = Hace viento
Wire = Alambre
Wire brush = Cepillo de
alambre
Wire Nut = Tuercade
alambre
With breakfast = Con el
desayuno
With dinner = Con la cena
With food = Con la
comida
With lunch = Con el
almuerzo
With milk = Con leche
With water = Con agua
Wood = Madera
Wood flooring = Piso de
madera
Wood screw = Tornillo
para madera
Worship = Adorar
Wound = Herido
Wrench = Llave de
tuercas
Wrist = Muñeca
Writing = Escribiendo

Y
Yellow = Amarillo
Yogurt = Yogurt
You (*informal*) = Tú
You (*Plural*) = Ustedes
You (*Polite*) = Usted

You are = Eres
You're welcome = De
nada.
Your = Tu, Tus

Spanish English
Dictionary

A
A la derecha =To the right
A la hora de acostarse =
At bedtime
A la izquierda = To the left
Abajo = Down
Abdomen = Abdomen
Abra = Open
Abre la boca. = Open your
mouth.
Abrigo = Overcoat
Abril = April
Absceso = Abscess
Ábside = Apse
Abuela = Grandmother
Abuelo = Grandfather
Acabado = Finish (wood)
Acabado liso = Smooth finish
Acabado ordinario = Rough
finish
Accesorios de drenaje =
Drainage fittings
Accidente = Accident
Aceptar = To accept
Acuéstese = Lie down.
Adelante = Straight ahead
Adentro = Inside
Adiós = Good-bye
Adorable = Adorable
Adorar = To worship
Adorar = Worship
Aduana = Customs
Aerolínea = Airline
Aeropuerto = Airport
Aeropuerto = Airport
Afuera = Outside
Agítese bien. = Shake well.

Agosto = August
Agotamiento de calor = Heat exhaustion
Agua = Water
Agua bendito = Holy Water
Agua negro = Sewage
Agua principal = Main water
Aguacate = Avocado
Ahora = Now
Ahora vengo = I'll be right back
Aislamiento = Insulation
Ajuste = Fitting
Al lado de = Beside
Alambrada = Chicken wire
Alambre = Wire
Alambre vivo = Live Wire
Albañal = Sewer
Albañil = Bricklayer
Alergias = Allergies
Alicates = Pliers
Allá = Over there
Allí = There
Almuerzo = Lunch
Altar = Altar
Alto voltaje = High voltage
Altura = Height
Amarillo = Yellow
Amarre = Cross bridging
Amígdala = Tonsil
Amor = Love
Amperímetro = Ammeter
Amperio = Ampere
Ampolla = Blister
Analgésico = Analgesic
Áncora = Anchors
Andamio = Scaffold
Andamio = Scaffold
Anemia = Anemia
Anestésico = Anesthetic
Ángel = Angel
Anillo = Ring
Animale = Animal
Animale de peluche = Stuffed animal
Ano = Anus
Ansiedad = Anxiety
Anteojos de seguridad, Gafas de protección = Safety glasses

Antes de las comidas = Before meals
Antiácido = Antacid
Antibiótico = Antibiotic
Anticoagulante = Anticoagulant
Antídoto = Antidote
Antihistamínicos = Antihistamine
Anti-inflamatorio = Anti-inflammatory
Antiséptico = Antiseptic
Antorcha de propano = Torch (propane)
Apellido = Last name (surname)
Apellido materno = Maternal surname
Apellido paterno = Paternal surname
Apéndice = Appendix
Apendicitis = Appendicitis
Apilar = Stack
Apio = Celery
Aplique = Apply
Apóstol = Apostle
Aquel, Aquellos, Aquella, Aquellas = That one over there
Aquí = Here
Arco = Arch
Área colectora = Drain area
Arena = Sand
Armadura de cubierto = Truss
Arnés = Harness
Arriba = Up
Arrodillarse = To kneel
Arroz = Rice
Artefacto = Fixture
Artefactos sanitarios = Plumbing fixtures
Artritis = Arthritis
Arzobispo = Archbishop
Así = Like this.
Así así = So so
Así no = Not like this.
Asiento = Seat
Asma = Asthma
Aspire profundo. = Take a deep breath.
Aspirina = Aspirin

Astringente = Astringent
Atril = Lectern
Atún = Tuna
Aumento de peso = Weight gain
Aumento del apetito = Increased appetite
Aureola = Halo
Autobús = Bus
Avenida = Avenue
Avión = Airplane
Ayudar = To help
Ayúdelo = Help him.
Ayúdeme = Help me.
Azadón = Hoe
Azul = Blue

B
Bajada de aguas = Downspout
Banco (*in church*) = Pew
Banco = Bank
Banqueta = Sidewalk
Baño, Servicio = Bathroom
Barandillas = Guardrail
Barbilla = Chin
Barbitúrico = Barbiturate
Barniz = Varnish
Barra = Crowbar
Barra de tierra = Ground Rod
Barrena = Auger
Barril = Barrel
Barrote dimensional = Dimensional lumber
Base = Primer
Basurero = Trash can
Bata = Robe
Bautizar = To baptize
Bautizar = To baptize
Bebida = Beverage
Bendición = Blessing
Biblia = Bible
Biblioteca = Library
Bien = Good.
Bistec = Steak
Blanco = White
Blasfemia = Blasphemy
Bloque de cemento = Cement block

Bloques de madera = Blocks
Boca = Mouth
Boca de admisión = Sewer tap
Boca seca = Dry mouth
Boleto = Ticket
Bolsa = Bag
Bomba = Pump
Bombilla, Foco = Bulb
Bonita = Pretty
Borde = Edge
Borde = Edger
Botas = Boots
Brazo = Arm
Brea = Tar
Brida = Flange
Broca = Drill bit
Brocha = Brush (paint)
Brócoli = Broccoli
Bronquitis = Bronchitis
Buena idea = Good idea.
Buenas noches = Good night
Buenas tardes = Good afternoon
Bueno = Good
Buenos días = Good morning
Bufanda = Scarf
Bulto = Lump

C
Caballo = Horse
Cabeza = Head
Cable = Cable
Cable de extensión = Extension cord
Cacerola = Pan
Café = Coffee
Café descafeinado = Decaffeinated coffee
Caídas = Falls
Caja = Box
Caja de mitra = Miter box
Calabacera = Squash
Calabaza = Pumpkin
Calafatear = Caulk
Calambre = Cramps
Calcetines = Socks
Cálculos en la vesícula = Gall stones

Cálculos en los riñones = Kidney stones
Calentador = Heater
Calentador de agua = Water Heater
Caliente = Hot
Cáliz = Chalice
Calle = Street
Cálmese = Calm down.
Calor = Hot
Cambio = Money exchange
Camisa = Shirt
Camiseta = T-shirt
Camote = Sweet potato
Campana = Bell
Campanario = Steeple
Canalón = Gutter
Cáncer = Cancer
Canciones = Songs
Cantar = To sing
Caoba = Mahogany
Capa = Course
Capellán = Chaplain
Capilla = Chapel
Capítulo = Chapter
Cápsula = Capsule
Cara = Face
Caretilla = Wheelbarrow
Carga = Load
Caridad = Charity
Carne = Meat
Carne de vaca = Beef
Carpintero = Joiner
Carro = Car
Cartas = Cards
Casco = Hard hat
Catarro = Cold
Catedral = Cathedral
Cebolla = Onion
Cedro = Cedar
Célula = Cell
Cena = Dinner
Cepillo de alambre = Wire brush
Cerámica = Tile (decorative)
Cerca de = Near
Cereal = Cereal
Cerebro = Brain
Cerezo = Cherry

Cerrajería = Hardware
Cerveza = Beer
Chaleco = Vest
Champiñón = Mushroom
Chapado = Veneer
Chaqueta = Jacket
Chicle = Chewing gum
Chistes = Jokes
Chistoso = Funny
Chocolate = Chocolate
Chuleta de puerco = Pork chop
Cielo = Heaven
Cierre = Close
Cincel = Chisel
Cine = Movie theatre
Cinta = Tape
Cinta para medir = Tape measure
Cinturón = Belt
Cinturón de seguridad = Safety belt
Cisterna = Toilet bowl
Claro = Light
Claro! = Sure
Clavos = Nails
Cloaca principal = Main sewer
Cobre = Copper
Coco = Coconut
Codeína = Codeine
Codo, Ele = Elbow
Colar = Pour
Coliflor = Cauliflower
Colón = Colon
Comida = Meal or food
Cómo = How
Cómo está = How are you
Cómo se dice en español = How do you say it in Spanish
Cómo se llama = What's your name
Cómo te llamas = What's your name
Comprende = Do you understand
Compresor = Compressor
Con agua = With water
Con el almuerzo = With lunch

139

Con el desayuno = With breakfast
Con el estómago vacío. = On an empty stomach
Con la cena = With dinner
Con la comida = With food
Con leche = With milk
Concreto = Concrete
Conducto de cable = Conduit (cable)
Conducto de Wharton = Wharton's duct
Conducto porta cables = Duct
Conducto, Tubo = Conduit (pipe)
Conector = Connector
Confesión = Confession
Confirmación = Confirmation
Contraceptivo = Contraceptive
Contramarcos = Trim
Contusión = Bruise
Convento = Convent
Corazón = Heart
Corbata = Tie
Coro = Choir Loft, Choir
Correo = Post office
Cortador = Cutter
Cortador de perforación = Hole Cutter
Cortar = Cut
Cortisona = Cortisone
Crema = Cream
Crema de cacahuate = Peanut butter
Crema de leche agria = Sour cream
Creo que sí = I believe so
Cristo = Christ
Crucero = Transept
Cruz = Cross
Cuál = Which or what
Cuándo = When
Cuánto = How much
Cuántos = How many
Cuántos años tienes = How old are you
Cubo = Bucket
Cuello = Neck
Cuentos = Stories

Cuerda = Rope
Cuerda para brincar = Jump rope
Cuerpo = Body
Cuezo = Hod
Cumbrera = Ridge board
Cuña = Wedge
Cuñada = Sister-in-law
Cuñado = Brother-in-law
Cura = Priest
Curva = Bend

D
Dama de honor = Bridesmaid
De acuerdo = I agree
De dónde es = Where are you from
De nada. = You're welcome
De veras = Really
Debajo = Under
Dedo = Finger
Dedo del pie = Toe
Démelo = Give it to me.
Dentro = Inside
Departamento de bomberos = Fire department
Depende. = That depends.
Deportes = Sports
Depósito = Bin
Desaforrar = Strip (Verb)
Desaguar = To drain
Desagüe = Drain
Desayuno = Breakfast
Desinfectante = Disinfectant
Después de las comidas = After meals
Destinación = Destination
Destornillador = Screwdriver
Destornillador de cruz = Screwdriver, Phillips
Destornillador plano = Screwdriver, flat
Desvístase = Get undressed.
Detector de humo = Smoke detector
Detrás = Behind
Diabetes = Diabetes
Diablo = Devil

140

Diácono = Deacon
Diafragma = Diaphragm
Diarrea = Diarrhea
Dibujando = Drawing
Diciembre = December
Diente = Tooth
Diente canino = Canine
Diente incisivo = Incisor
Dientes = Teeth
Diluyente = Thinner
Díme = Tell me.
Dios te bendiga = God bless you
Dios, Señor = God
Dirección = Address
Director del coro = Choir director
Discípulo = Disciple
Disminución del apetito = Decreased appetite
Distendidas = Strained
Diurético = Diuretic
Doble = Turn
Dolor = In pain.
Dolor = Pain
Dolor constante = Constant pain
Dolor de cabeza = Headache
Dolor intermitente = Intermittent pain
Dolor moderado = Mild pain
Dolor muy fuerte = Severe pain
Dolor profundo = Deep pain
Dolor pulsante = Throbbing pain
Dolor quemante = Burning pain
Domingo = Sunday
Dónde = Where
Dónde = Where
Dónde está = Where is...
Dónde vives = Where do you live
Drenaje, Desagüe = Drainage
Dulce = Candy

E
Edad = Age
Ejote = Green bean

Él = He
El (m), La (f) = The *(Singular)*
El gusto es mío = The pleasure is mine.
Electricidad = Electricity
Electrocución = Electrocution
Ella = She
Ellos, Ellas *(f)* = They
Empalmar = Splice
En frente de = In front of
En los áreas afectados = To affected areas
Encías = Gums
Encima = Above
Enero = January
Engrapadora = Stapler
Enladrillar = Brick up
Enladrillar = Lay
Ensalada = Salad
Entablado de muro = Wall sheathing
Entablando de techo = Roof sheathing
Entre las comidas = Between meals
Equipaje de mano = Carry on baggage
Eres = You are
Erupción = Rash
Es grave. = It's serious.
Es importante = It's important
Es posible = It's possible.
Escalera de mano = Ladder
Escalofrío = Chills
Escarbador de Juntas = Jointer
Escoba = Broom
Escribiendo = Writing
Escuela = School
Ese, Esa = That
Esófago = Esophagus
Esos, Esas = Those
Espalda = Back
Espátula angosta = Putty knife
Espere = Wait
Espina = Spine
Espíritu Santo = Holy Spirit
Esposa = Wife
Esposo = Husband

Está bien = That's OK
Está seguro *(a)* = Are you sure
Estación de autobuses = Bus station
Estación de policía = Police station
Estación de tren = Train station
Estación de tren = Train station
Este = East
Este, Esta = This
Esteroide = Steroid
Estómago = Stomach
Estos, Estas = These
Estreñimiento = Constipation
Estructura = Framing
Estuco = Stucco
Eterno = Eternal
Evangelio = Gospel
Evangelista = Evangelist
Excavación = Excavation
Excelente = Excellent
Excelente = Excellent
Exponer = Exposed
Extensión eléctrica = Electric cord
Exterior = Exterior
Externamente = Externally
Extinguidor de fuego = Fire extinguisher

F
Falda = Skirt
Fantástico = Fantastic
Farmacia = Pharmacy
Febrero = February
Fecha de nacimiento = Date of birth
Feliz cumpleaños = Happy birthday
Fiebre = Fever
Fiebre de heno = Hay fever
Fieles = Congregation
Fieltro de techar = Felt
Fiestas = Parties
Fila = Row
Flan = Custard
Flauta = Flute
Florería = Florist

Flores = Flowers
Flotador = Float
Flujo = Flow
Fluorescente = Fluorescent
Fracturas = Fractures
Fregadero = Kitchen sink
Fresa = Strawberry
Frijoles = Dried Beans
Frijoles negros = Black beans
Frío = Cold
Fruta = Fruit
Fuego = Fire
Fundación = Foundation
Fusible = Fuse

G
Galleta = Cookie
Galleta salada = Cracker
Garganta = Throat
Gasolinera = Gas station
Gatos = Cats
Glaucoma = Glaucoma
Globos = Balloons
Golpeadas = Bruised
Goma = Glue
Gota = Drop (liquid)
Gotero = Drip
Gracias por su paciencia. = Thanks for your patience.
Gracias = Thank you.
Gramo = Gram
Grampa = Ground Clamp
Grande = Big
Granito = Granite
Grapas = Staples
Grava = Gravel
Grifo = Faucet
Gris = Gray
Grosería = Grocery store
Guantes = Gloves
Guapo = Handsome
Guarda en el refrigerador. = Keep refrigerated.
Guisantes = Green peas
Guitarra = Guitar

142

H

Habla inglés = Do you speak English
Habla más despacio = Speak more slowly.
Hablo poco español = I speak a little Spanish.
Hace buen tiempo = Nice weather
Hace calor = Hot weather
Hace fresco = Cool
Hace frío = Cold weather
Hace sol = Sunny weather
Hace viento = Windy
Hacha = Ax
Hambre = Hungry
Hamburguesa = Hamburger
Helado = Ice-cream
Hepatitis = Hepatitis
Hereje = Heretic
Herejía = Heresy
Herido = Wound
Hermana = Sister
Hermano = Brother
Herpes = Herpes
Herramienta = Tool
Hierro = Iron
Hierro fundido = Cast iron
Hígado = Liver
Hija = Daughter
Hijo = Son
Hilera = Row / line
Hilera de ladrillos = Soldier course
Himnario = Hymn book
Hinchazón = Bump
Hipoglucemia = Hypoglycemia
Hoja de sierra = Saw blade
Hola = Hi
Hombro = Shoulder
Hormigón en bloques = Precast
Hospital = Hospital
Hostia = Consecrated wafer
Hotel = Hotel
Hueso roto = Broken bone
Huevo = Egg
Huevo duro = Hard-boiled egg
Huevo revuelto = Scrambled egg

I

Ictericia = Jaundice
Iglesia = Church
Impermeable = Raincoat
Incandescente = Incandescent
Incienso = Incense
Inclinación = Slope
Indícalo. = Show me.
Indigestión = Indigestion
Indíquelo = Point to it.
Infierno = Hell
Inflamación = Swelling
Influenza = Flu
Inhalador = Inhaler
Inquieto = Restless
Insomnio = Insomnia
Insulina = Insulin
Interior = Interior
Interruptor = Switch
Interruptor automático,
Cortacircuito = Circuit Breaker
Intestino delgado = Small intestine
Intestino grueso = Large intestine
Inyectar lechada = Grout

J

Jamón = Ham
Jaqueca, Migraña = Migraine
Jarabe para la tos = Cough syrup
Jeans, Vaqueros = Jeans
Jesús = Jesus
Joyería = Jewelry store
Juego de damas = Checkers
Juegos = Games
Jueves = Thursday
Jugar = To play
Jugo = Juice
Juguetes = Toys
Julio = July
Junio = June
Junta de cemento = Spackle

K

Kilo = Kilo

143

L

Ladrillo = Brick
Ladrillo a tizón = Header
Ladrillo aislador = Insulating brick
Ladrillo al hilo = Stretcher
Ladrillo alivianado = Hollow brick
Ladrillo de concreto = Concrete brick
Ladrillo de cuello = Neck brick
Ladrillo de fachada = Face brick
Ladrillo de fuego = Fire brick
Ladrillo de jamba = Jamb brick
Ladrillo liso = Smooth brick
Ladrillos a canto = Brick laid on edge
Ladrillos a sardinel = Rowlock
Ladrillos de testa = Brick laid on end
Lámina = Sheeting
Lápices de color = Crayons
Lápiz = Pencil
Largo = Length
Laringitis = Laryngitis
Lata = Can
Lavabo = Lavatory
Lavabo pedestal = Pedestal sink
Lavandería = Laundromat
Laxante = Laxative
Le respeto. = I respect you.
Lechada = Grout
Leche = Milk
Leche con crema = Half and half
Leche sin grasa = Non-fat milk
Lechuga = Lettuce
Lejos = Far
Lengua = Tongue
Leucemia = Leukemia
Levantamiento = Lifting
Levantar = To lift
Levántese = Stand up
Leyendo = Reading
Libra = Pound
Libros = Books
Líder = Leader

Lijadora = Sander
Lima = Lime
Lima = File
Limón = Lemon
Limpiar = Clean
Línea = Line
Línea de tiza = Chaulk line
Linimento = Liniment
Linóleo = Linoleum
Liso = Smooth
Litro = Liter
Llamar = To call
Llana = Trowel
Llave de tuercas = Wrench
Llegada = Arrival
Llevar = To carry
Lleve esto. = Carry this.
Llover = To rain
Lluvia = Rain
Loción = Lotion
Lodo = Mud
Lona = Canvas or tarp
Losa = Slab
Lubricante = Lubricant
Lugar de nacimiento = Place of birth
Lunes = Monday
Luz = Light
Luz fluorescente = Fluorescent light

M

Madera = Wood
Madera aserradas = Sawn timber
Madera de construcción = Lumber
Madera dura = Hard wood
Madera laminada = Plywood
Madre = Mother
Madrina = Godmother
Maíz = Corn
Mal = Bad
Mala reacción = Bad reaction
Mango = Mango
Manguera = Hose
Manguito = Sleeve
Mano = Hand

144

Manteca = Lard
Mantequilla = Butter
Manzana = Apple
Máquina = Machine
Mareos, Vértigo = Dizziness
Mariscos = Seafood
Marro = Sledgehammer
Marrón = Brown
Martes = Tuesday
Martillo = Hammer
Martillo de enladrillador = Brick hammer
Marzo = March
Más = More
Más o menos. = More or less
Más tarde = Later.
Masa de yeso = Joint compound
Masilla = Putty
Mastique = Mastic
Mayo = May
Mazo = Mallet
Me alegro = I'm so glad
Me llamo = My name is
Medio = Half
Melocotón = Peach
Melón, Cantalupo = Cantaloupe
Membrana = Membrane
Menos = Less
Mercado = Market
Merienda = Snack
Mermelada = Jam
Metal corrugado = Corrugated metal
Metro = Subway
Mezclador de mortero = Mortar mixer
Mezclar = Mix
Mi, Mis = My
Miedo de = Afraid of
Miel = Honey
Miércoles = Wednesday
Milagro = Miracle
Mililitro = Milliliter
Ministro = Minister
Misa = Mass
Moho = Mildew
Monasterio = Monastery

Monja = Nun
Monje = Monk
Mono = Cute
Montantes de acero = Steel studs
Montantes de madera = Stud (wooden)
Montañas = Mountains
Morado = Purple
Moreno = Brown
Morfina = Morphine
Mucho gusto! = Nice to meet you.
Muela, Molar = Molar
Muéstreme = Show me.
Mueve eso aquí = Move that here.
Municipio = City hall
Muñeca = Wrist, or Dolls
Muro de ladrillos = Brick wall
Museo = Museum
Música = Music
Muy bien = Very good!
Muy importante = Very important!

N

Nacionalidad = Nationality
Naranja = Orange
Narcótico = Narcotic
Nariz = Nose
Navaja = Knife
Nave = Nave
Nave lateral = Aisle
Necesitar = To need
Negro = Black
Neutral = Neutral
Nieta = Granddaughter
Nieto = Grandson
Niño (a) = Child
Nitroglicerina = Nitroglycerine
Nivel = Level
No comprendo. = I don't understand.
No fumar = No smoking.
Nombre completo = Full name
Nombre de esposo (a) = Name of husband/wife

Nombre de niño = Name of child
Norte = North
Nos vemos. = We'll see you.
Nosotros, Nosotras *(f)* = We
Novia = Bride
Noviembre = November
Novio = Groom
Nuera = Daughter-in-law
Nuestro (-os), Nuestra (-as) = Our
Nuevo = New
Número de teléfono de su casa = Home telephone number

O
Obispo = Bishop
Octubre = October
Oeste = West
Oferta = Offering
Ofertorio = Offertory
Oficina de objetos perdidos = Lost and found
Ojo = Eye
Oración = Prayer
Oreja = Ear
Orificio de purga = Drain hole
Orificio de ventilación = Vent
Oscuro = Dark

P
Padre = Father
Padrino = Godfather
Pagano = Non-believer
Pájaros = Birds
Pala = Shovel
Paladar blando = Soft palate
Paladar duro = Hard palate
Pan = Bread
Panadería = Bakery
Panel de rompedores = Breaker Panel
Paneles = Paneling
Pantalones = Pants
Pantalones cortos = Shorts
Papa = Pope

Papaya = Papaya
Papel de brea = Tarpaper
Papel de lija = Sand paper
Paperas = Mumps
Para uso externo = For external use
Parábola = Parable
Paraguas = Umbrella
Parar = Stop
Parche = Patch
Pare = Stop.
Pared = Wall
Pared de carga = Bearing wall
Parque = Park
Parroquia = Parish
Pasillo = Aisle
Pasita = Raisin
Pastel, Queque = Cake
Pastilla = Lozenge
Pastillas para la tos = Cough drop
Pastor *(a)* = Pastor
Patata = Potato
Pavo = Turkey
Pecado = Sin
Pecho = Chest
Peligro = Danger!
Peluquería = Barber shop
Penicilina = Penicillin
Pepino = Cucumber
Pequeño = Little
Pera = Pear
Perdón = Excuse me.
Peregrino = Pilgrim
Perforación = Hole
Perforar = Drill
Perno = Bolt
Perro caliente = Hot Dog
Perro = Dog
Pescado = Fish
Pez = Fish
Piadoso = Pious
Picazón = Itching
Pico = Pick
Pie = Foot
Piedad = Piety
Piedra = Rock
Piedra = Stone
Piel = Skin

Pierna = Leg
Pijamas = Pajamas
Pila = Font
Pila = Basin
Pila bautismal = Baptismal font
Píldora = Pill
Pimiento verde = Green bell pepper
Pintar = Coloring/painting
Pintura = Paint
Pinza = Clamp
Piña = Pineapple
Piso = Floor
Piso de madera = Wood flooring
Pistola de clavos, Pistola = Nail gun
Pistola de pegamento = Glue gun
Pizarra = Slate
Plancha de escurrimiento = Flashing
Plancha de soldar = Soldering iron
Plano = Plane
Plataforma = Platform
Plátano = Banana
Platillos = Cymbals
Playa = Beach
Plomero = Plumber
Pollo = Chicken
Póngalo allí = Put it there.
Poquito = A tiny amount
Por favor! = Please!
Por la mañana = In the morning
Por la noche = In the evening
Por la tarde = In the afternoon
Por qué = Why
Pórtico = Porch
Postre = Dessert
Precioso = Precious
Predicar = To preach
Preguntar = To ask
Preparar = To prepare
Presión = Pressure
Presión sanguínea alta = High blood pressure
Presión sanguínea baja = Low blood pressure

Primer nombre = First name
Primera comunión = First communion
Primeros auxilios = First aid
Primo (a) = Cousin
Profundidad = Depth
Promesas solemnes = Vows
Propano = Propane
Propano = Propane
Protección = Protection
Pudín = Pudding
Pulmón = Lung
Pulmonía = Pneumonia
Púlpito = Pulpit

Q
Qué = What
Qué pasa = What's happening
Qué tiempo hace = What's the weather
Quemadura = Burn
Queso = Cheese
Quién = Who
Quimioterapia = Chemotherapy
Quite estos = Remove these.
Quizás = Maybe

R
Raspador = Scraper
Raspar = Scrape
Rastrillo = Rake
Razón = Right
Receptáculo, Caja de contacto = Receptacle
Receta médica, Fórmula, = Prescription
Reclamo de equipaje = Barrage claim
Recoja todo estos = Pick up all these.
Recto = Rectum
Redondo = Round
Reforzado = Reinforce
Refresco dieta = Diet soda
Refresco, Soda = Soft drink
Regla = Ruler

Regresar = To return
Repita por favor = Repeat please.
Reserva = Reservation
Resina = Resin
Respire profundo. = Breathe deeply.
Restaurante = Restaurant
Rezar = To pray
Riñón = Kidney
Riostra = Brace
Ripia = Shingle
Roble dorado = Golden oak
Rodilla = Knee
Rojo = Red
Rollo = Roll
Rompecabezas = Puzzles
Ronchas de la piel = Hives
Ropa interior = Underwear
Rosa = Pink
Rosario = Rosary
Rosca de tubería = Pipe Threader

S
Sábado = Saturday
Sacando clavos = Pulling nails
Sacristía = Vestry
Salchicha = Sausage
Salida = Departure/Exit/Gate
Salmo = Psalm
Salón de belleza = Beauty salon
Sandalias = Sandals
Sandía = Watermelon
Sándwich = Sandwich
Sangrado = Bleeding
Sangre = Blood
Santidad = Holiness
Santo
Santa = Saint
Santuario = Sanctuary
Sarampión = Measles
Secar = Set up (dry)
Sed = Thirsty
Sedante = Sedative

Según las instrucciones de su doctor. = As directed by your doctor
Segundo nombre = Middle name
Seguridad = Security
Seguro = Safe
Sellador = Caulk
Sellador de silicón = Silicone sealant
Selva = Jungle
Señor = Sir or Mister
Señora = Mrs. or Ma'am
Señorita = Miss
Septiembre = September
Sermón = Sermon
Serrucho eléctrico = Power saw
Serrucho, Sierra = Saw
Servicio = Service
Siempre = Forever
Siéntese = Sit down
Sierra para cortar metal = Hack saw
Silicón = Silicone
Simpático = Nice
Sistema de drenaje = Drain system
Soldadura = Solder
Solo cuando es necesario = Only when necessary
Solo cuando tiene dolor = Only when you have pain
Solución = Solution
Sombrero = Hat
Sopa = Soup
Soporte = Sill
Sotana = Cassock
Su, Sus = His, her or Your (polite)
Súbase = Get up
Súbase a la mesa = Get up on the table.
Subsuelo = Sub floor
Suegra = Mother-in-law
Suegro = Father-in-law
Sueño = Sleepy
Suéter = Sweater
Super Mercado = Super market

Supositorios = Suppositories
Sur = South

T
Tabla de madera = Board
Tableta = Tablet
Tablón = Plank
Tachón = Stud
Taco, Clavija = Dowel
Taladro = Drill
Tamarindo = Tamarind
Tambor = Drum
Tanque de sanitario = Toilet
tank
Tapa = Cover
Tapón = Plug
Tapón de evacuación = Drain
plug
Tarta = Pie
Taxi = Taxi
Té = Tea
Te gusta.... = Do you like....
Teatro = Theatre
Techo = Ceiling
Teja = Tile (roofing)
Tela = Fabric
Tenga cuidado. = Be careful.
Tenga un buen día = Have a
nice day
Tenis = Sneakers
Teología = Theology
Terminal = Terminal
Termostato = Thermostat
Tía = Aunt
Tienda = Store
Tierra = Ground
Tijeras = Scissors
Tímido = Shy
Tinta = Stain
Tío = Uncle
Tira de borde = Edge strips
Tobillo = Ankle
Tocando música = Playing
music
Toma = Take
Tomate = Tomato
Torcedura = Sprain
Tornillo de banco = Vise

Tornillo para madera = Wood
screw
Tornillo = Screw
Toronja = Grapefruit
Tortilla de huevos = Omelet
Tortuga = Turtle
Tos = Cough
Tostaditas = Chips
Trabajar = To work
Tráigame eso = Bring me that.
Traje = Suit
Traje de baño = Bathing suit
Trampa = Trap
Tranquilizantes = Tranquilizers
Tranquilo = Calm
Transportación =
Transportation
Trapeador = Mop
Trapo = Cloth
Travesaño = Header
Tú = You (informal)
Tu, Tus = Your
Tuberculosis = Tuberculosis
Tubo = Pipe
Tubo de desagüe = Drain pipe
Tuercas = Nuts

# U
Umbral = Sill
Uña = Nail
Urticaria = Hives
Usar = To use
Usted = You (Polite)
Ustedes = You (Plural)
Uva = Grape
Úvula = Uvula

# V
Vacuna = Vaccine
Válvula = Valve
Válvula de cierre, Válvula de
interrupción = Shut off
Válvula purgadora de
sedimentos = Drain valve
Vámonos = Let's go.
Varicela = Chicken pox

Varilla = Rebar
Vatios = Watts
Véase = Gauge
Vegetales = Vegetables
Ven aquí. = Come here.
Venga aquí = Come here.
Ventana = Window
Ventilador de ático = Attic fan
Ventilador de techo =
Ceiling fan
Verde = Green
Vergüenza = Ashamed
Verso = Verse
Vesícula billar = Gall bladder
Vestíbulo = Vestibule
Vestido = Dress
Vestiduras = Vestments
Veta = Grain
Viaje de misión = Mission trip
Vidriera = Stained glass
Viejo = Old
Viernes = Friday
Viga = Beam
Viga de entre piso = Floor joist
Viga horizontal = Plate
Viga principal = Girder
Villancico = Carol
Vino blanco = White wine
Vino tinto = Red wine
Vitamina = Vitamin
Voltéese = Turn around.
Voltímetro = Voltmeter
Vuelto = Flight

Y
Ya me voy = I'm leaving now
Yerno = Son-in-law
Yeso = Plaster
Yo = I
Yo también. = Me, too
Yo tampoco. = Me, neither
Yogurt = Yogurt

# Z
Zanahoria = Carrot
Zanja = Trench
Zapatería = Shoe store
Zapatos = Shoes

About the Author

Myelita Melton, founder of SpeakEasy Communications, remembers the first time she heard a "foreign" language. She knew from that moment what she wanted to do with her life. "Since I was always the kid in class that talked too much," Myelita says, "I figured it would be a good idea to learn more than one language—that way I could talk to more people!"

She has studied in Saltillo, Mexico at the *Instituto de Filológica Hispánica* and completed both her BA and MA in at Appalachian State University in Boone, NC.

"Lita's" unique career includes classroom instruction and challenging corporate experience. She has won several national awards, including a prestigious *Rockefeller* scholarship and in 1994 she was named to *Who's Who Among Outstanding Americans.* Myelita's corporate experience includes owning a television production firm, working with NBC's Spanish news division, *Canal de Noticias,* and Charlotte's PBS affiliate. In her spare time, she continues to broadcast with WDAV, a National Public Radio affiliate near Lake Norman in North Carolina where she lives.

Currently, Myelita enjoys traveling and providing programs on Spanish language qcquisition and diversity issues at a variety of national conventions each year. In the future, she will be designing e-learning courses which will be offered at the company's website. Visit www.SpeakEasySpanish.com to read Myelita's latest articles or to inquire about her on-site programs.

CPSIA information can be obtained at www.ICGtesting.com
Printed in the USA
LVOW07s1001100913

351665LV00014B/333/P